Forever Sweethearts

Forever Sweethearts

Sixty Years of Love, Life & Laughter in Liverpool

JUNE BERNICOFF

BLINK

bringing you closer

Published by Blink Publishing
2.25, The Plaza,
535 Kings Road,
Chelsea Harbour,
London, SW10 0SZ

www.blinkpublishing.co.uk

facebook.com/blinkpublishing
twitter.com/blinkpublishing

Hardback – 978-1-788-700-92-4
Trade paperback – 978-1-788-700-93-1
Paperback – 978-1-788-701-70-9
Ebook – 978-1-788-701-45-7

A CIP catalogue of this book is available from the British Library.

Typeset by seagulls.net
Printed and bound in Great Britain by Clays Ltd, Elcograf S.p.A.

1 3 5 7 9 10 8 6 4 2

Copyright © June Bernicoff, 2018
First published by Blink Publishing in 2018
This edition first published by Blink Publishing in 2019

Blink Publishing is an imprint of Bonnier Books UK
www.bonnierbooks.co.uk

To Leon, my husband, my best friend, my soulmate and sparring partner, who shared my innermost secrets and taught me to live every day to the full.

To my wonderful family, always planning something for me to aim for and helping me adjust to this new chapter in my life.

Contents

Preface

As anyone who has watched Channel 4's *Gogglebox* will know, my husband Leon loved telling stories. In fact, in 1999 he published a children's book, *Tiger And Fudge*, where the stories themselves revolved around the lives of our daughters, Helen and Julie, and their pet cats (who gave the book its name). In the wake of that book, we often tried to persuade him to write another. He always replied that one day he would: it would be our story or, indeed, our 'love story', as he put it. As a result, when I was approached to write this book, following Leon's passing in December 2017, it felt somehow fitting. I needed some kind of challenge to focus on, something positive, and writing our story offered me that and gave me time to reflect on things.

I believe that I was blessed to have had a very long and happy marriage with a truly remarkable man, without whom I would never have achieved the things I did in life. Leon gave me the confidence to grasp every opportunity, to live every moment, and to enjoy it all. Certainly, without him, I would never have taken part in *Gogglebox*. In hindsight, it was the most unexpected and utterly unique opportunity, and we both thoroughly enjoyed it. In fact, the programme itself became such a huge part of our lives, and I think we both felt very grateful for that.

Of course, Leon would have loved to have written this book. It would have been very different, had he done so. He would undoubtedly have taken a no-holds-barred approach to writing it, especially when it came to details of our courtship. I dare say that it may well have been a little bit more explicit! It may also have been funnier and, somehow, louder too. And, needless to say, by the final page we would have had precious few family secrets left.

But among these acts of sheer literary recklessness, Leon would also have stressed one key point: if you are fortunate to find someone you love, someone with whom you want to share the rest of your life, then you will find a way for that to happen. Race, culture and religion are not barriers in those circumstances, they are simply hurdles to be overcome. In life, the qualities of love, laughter and happiness are the most important things of all. I have been fortunate to enjoy a lifetime filled with all of these things, thanks to Leon and our family, and this is what this book is about. I hope you enjoy it.

June Bernicoff, September 2018

CHAPTER 1

'We're going to be on telly, June!'

'June! June! Wait until you hear the news! We're going to be on television!' exclaimed Leon as he burst through the front door on what was a relatively warm Tuesday afternoon in spring 2012. As usual, he'd just been to play bridge with his friend Peter and, to be honest, I knew something was up as soon as I heard him pull up in the driveway.

Despite having driven for over 60 years, Leon could never park a car properly. Having passed his test the third time, he seemed to have constant issues with spatial awareness and would park either right against the wall of our house, or a good metre away. The running joke in our family revolved around the fact that, one day, he'd come crashing through the front of the house and end up parking the car in the middle of our dining room.

Normally, Leon would announce his arrival by furiously parping the horn. As soon as I appeared at the doorway, he'd stop and I would help to make sure the car was parked properly. This time, however, our trusty Ford Ghia would remain at an obscure angle, almost abandoned in the driveway, as he rang the doorbell frantically.

When I answered the door, he bundled past me, seemingly in a desperate rush. At first, I thought he'd had another argument with one of his fellow players, something that wasn't entirely uncommon, quite often because Leon would get told off for chatting when he should have been concentrating fully on the game. Either that, or this was an obvious display of joy relating to a magnificent victory. The idea of us appearing on television was not, however, something that had crossed my mind. Ever. Leon's enthusiasm, though, was palpable, his grin spreading from ear to ear, as I walked back into the kitchen to continue chopping vegetables.

'Did you hear what I said?' he asked, with a slight air of agitation in his voice.

'Yes. Apparently, we're going to be on television,' I answered. I must've sounded distinctly unimpressed because Leon harrumphed and then redoubled his enthusiasm.

'Yes! Television, June!' he continued. 'Two lovely girls walked into bridge today and they want us to appear on television!'

'Oh, two lovely girls asked you, did they?' I countered.

'Yes, It's for a new show! Mission accomplished!' he smiled.

'Leon,' I said. 'What *are* you talking about? People like us aren't on television.'

He fell silent and went to hang his coat up. Clearly, I'd already poured cold water on the entire situation. When he came back, he looked at me with a slightly hurt expression as I carried on chopping.

'We *are* going to be on television. We're going to be famous. You and me, June. Not Peter and I, you and me,' he insisted, in what was almost a whisper.

* * *

Like most things he did in life, when Leon decided to start playing bridge, he threw himself into it furiously. He had played the card game socially and intermittently for many years but when he retired in 1989, he elected to learn to play it 'properly'. Of course he was determined to have lessons to ensure he stood a chance of winning from Day One, and he was taught by someone who was eminently suited to him: Ivy Blackwell, whom he greatly admired as a teacher and as a person. Bridge became one of his great passions and, after 12 months of playing at different venues and clubs (one of which he helped run for a while), he finally joined Liverpool Bridge Club in late 1990.

There, his long-suffering friend, Peter Armstrong, became his playing partner ten years later.

Leon first met Peter, who was a few years his junior, in 1966 when they were teachers at Gateacre School, the secondary school which was located to the south-east of Liverpool. Peter was tall, dark, slim and, like Leon, fiercely competitive. The difference between them was that Peter liked to play by the rules; Leon, however, delighted in breaking them. At Gateacre, they forged a lasting alliance, becoming Everton Football Club season ticket holders and then shareholders, all while following the club around the country. They also became golfing partners and, in later life, they graduated to playing bridge – a pastime that should possibly have been less stressful than football or even golf, but which, thanks to Leon's approach, was nothing of the sort.

Tuesdays and Thursdays were designated afternoons spent at Liverpool Bridge Club, an establishment that was run by Ivy herself, who also acted as Leon's mentor. It was Ivy, in fact, who introduced Leon to two young ladies from a television company, who had wandered into the club that Tuesday afternoon. According to her, they had come up to Liverpool for a few days to cast for a new television series and they'd dropped into the club in search of 'normal' people.

Ivy had explained this to Leon and, without hesitation, he'd volunteered to get involved. When he told me, I was quite shocked that he had. Then again, Leon always loved the limelight. I had known that from the day I first met him, back in 1955, but this situation seemed a bit rash even by his standards.

Once I'd finished preparing dinner, we repaired to our sitting room with a cup of tea, and it was clear that I hadn't actually managed to dampen Leon's enthusiasm after all. He seemed completely oblivious to the fact that he was clearly just one of many people that the casting team had approached to appear on their programme. Nor did he seem to realise that nothing had actually been agreed at this stage. Later, we would find out that the show itself had yet to be commissioned, and when they began the casting process, the very idea of the programme was at an embryonic stage. But none of this seemed to matter to Leon. He had already made up his mind: a glorious future on the small screen awaited!

'The production company are going to ring us in the next 24 hours,' he continued excitedly.

In fact, following a quick phone call the very next day, 48 hours later, two members of the production team from a company called Studio Lambert were sitting in our front room, filming us as they showed us a series of photographs of assorted public figures and asked us what thoughts sprang to mind. Leon was his typical buoyant self, his voice rising with excitement at times as he talked for England about any subject put before him. For the most part I sat back and looked at him: he really was in his element.

They talked us through the premise of this new show: we would be filmed in our sitting room watching a number of television programmes every week. There would be other families involved, and we would be intercut with them. Our collective opinions would provide a review of the preceding week's programmes and the latest news stories. That was it. If I'm honest, it all sounded rather simplistic.

After two hours or so, the production team left, armed with footage of us to show the executive producer, Tania Alexander, back in London. By this point, Leon's excitement was almost at fever pitch. He reached for the phone and began ringing all and sundry to inform them of what had happened. Our eldest daughter Helen who lives a couple hours away from us in Kenilworth was first on the list.

'Mum! Please don't let Dad appear on television! You know what he'll be like!' Helen said when she finally spoke to me.

Our youngest daughter, Julie, was a lot more relaxed. Quite possibly because she lives in New Zealand.

'I'm 11,000 miles away, so as far as I'm concerned, you can both do what you like!' she laughed. In fact, the only time she seemed to object was when Leon – forgetting the time difference – rang her in the middle of the night in a fit of sheer excitement and began to discuss our screen test.

The girls and our close friends were not the only people subject to his surfeit of sheer enthusiasm. There were moments when Leon would randomly wake in the middle of the night and wake me up too.

'We're going to be on telly, June!' he'd roar.

'Stop it, Leon!' I'd say. 'This might never happen! Now, go back to sleep.'

And, of course, for a while, it didn't happen at all. It was a good few weeks later, around the beginning of May 2012, by the time we heard back from Studio Lambert again. This time they said they wanted to come and film us for what was effectively a pilot. And so they visited us again later that month, and filmed us in our lounge as we watched a number of programmes, including Channel 4's *Embarrassing Bodies* and ITV's *The Voice* – which was presented at the time by Holly Willoughby, and for whom Leon reserved some choice words.

'She got good legs!' he observed.

'Stop it, Leon!' I squirmed.

'You see? You see what she's like?' he laughed. And the crew laughed with him.

On reflection, they probably thought we were something of a bizarre double act. At the time, though, I couldn't for the life of me understand why they would want us to appear on television. It seemed totally absurd.

* * *

Gogglebox. When I first heard the name, I thought it was plain ridiculous. Of course, it's an expression for a television set, but it had been years since I'd heard anyone refer to a TV in that way. That's how old-fashioned it seemed. Then, there was the very idea that people would be willing to watch a couple in their mid- and late-seventies discussing the shows they'd watched that week. Who in their right mind would really want to watch that?

Having spent years sitting and watching television in our lounge together, I was also slightly worried that the appeal of Leon's verbal outbursts might be rather limited. Was there *really* an audience out there willing to tolerate him randomly calling someone a 'dickhead!' as he was prone to doing on occasion? The thought of it horrified me, I could think of nothing worse. Leon, however, had different ideas. Eight months had passed since we'd filmed what they had called the 'proof-of-concept' tape. We had received a call from Tania Alexander at the end of 2012, who told us that the show had been commissioned and they definitely wanted us to be a part of it. A contract duly arrived in the post and, being blunt, I was fairly adamant that I did not want to sign it.

While I continued to prevaricate, Leon used his considerable powers of persuasion to convince me that doing the show was a fantastic idea. The turning point came when he reminded me of something my father used to say: 'Remember, you may never pass this way again.' Whenever I was in doubt, I'd hear him saying those words. It was his way of telling me to seize every opportunity and damn the consequences! Remembering that phrase is what finally convinced me to sign up.

In February 2013, we met the production crew, who told us the series would be broadcast in March. They were very enthusiastic about our involvement, so that made me feel a little more comfortable, too. The fact that they said the show would be on late at night added further reassurance to the situation. It was due to be transmitted on a Thursday night at 10pm, and in my mind, that meant no one would ever actually get to see the programme. Certainly, no one *we* knew.

The fact that there were only four shows in the series also meant that it would probably all be forgotten about in the space of a month and we could go back to living our lives undisturbed. Little did we know what the programme would become and how much our lives would in fact change. How could we? Like I said, people like us weren't the sort of people who appeared on television. We were ordinary people, living an ordinary life, and we had been happy doing so since we'd got married back in the summer of 1960.

CHAPTER 2

. . . .

Meeting Leon

CHAPTER 2

Meeting Leon

*L*eon and I first met when we both arrived at Alsager Teacher Training College in Cheshire, in September 1955. I was 18 years old and he was about to turn 21. It was Freshers' Week at the college and my friend Glenda – who I had known since the age of five – was with me. She was studying History and I was studying English and Music. One evening, during that first week, I walked into the college lounge and found Glenda talking with a group of her fellow History students. History was, and still is, a subject that I have never enjoyed, so I ignored the conversation and sat on the edge of this fairly large group of people. One of the members of this gang seemed to notice my reticence and leant over to talk to me.

'Do you smoke?' he asked, offering Glenda and I a cigarette. I looked up at this man and, framed under an unruly head of hair that sat atop his short back and sides, I noticed his rather broad smile. In his hand he held a packet of 20 Senior Service cigarettes. Glenda and I were immediately impressed – we could just about afford a packet of ten and we had to club together to buy those. I also noticed that he was really well dressed. While most of the students were loafing about in jeans and fishermen's sweaters, he had a sports coat on, smart trousers and a shirt and tie. I looked at his right hand and noticed he was also wearing a signet ring – he was clearly a man of means. He was also incredibly well spoken, his accent the product of his education at the celebrated King's School in Chester, which, to use one of his favourite *Gogglebox* put-downs, made him something of a 'posh boy'.

'Hello, I'm Les,' he said, introducing himself. At the time, of course, I had no idea his real name was Leon, and that he'd decided to use another name. Later on, it became clear that he'd done so because as a child he'd been made to feel different. His real name – Leon Bernicoff – was different. His Jewish ancestry was different. The fact that he lived above a lady's gown shop that his parents ran was different. In his mind, all of these things had set him apart and he'd tried to remedy that by becoming more 'ordinary'. The irony in all of this was that on that September afternoon, as far as I was concerned, Leon most definitely stood apart: he was wonderfully different.

I noticed that although everybody was talking, Leon seemed to have the ability to command attention. He had this deep voice and *that* smile that was also very much his own. He began telling Glenda and I about his time as a gunner in the army, and when he'd been confined to barracks for staying out all night, plus his taste for blue cheese – most particularly Stilton and Danish Blue. *Blue cheese?* I barely knew what blue cheese was. And, again, I was impressed by this man who seemed to embody a sense of sophistication that I – having grown up in Tredegar, South Wales – hadn't quite experienced before.

After that first encounter, Leon, Glenda and I met several times in the college lounge. If there were no tutorials, we'd meet up between 4:30pm and 6pm, so that was the time during which we would socialise. He and Glenda seemed to get on very well and I thought that he was attracted to her at first. She was extremely attractive, with dark brown hair and dark eyes, and with an almost Italian elegance about her. 'She's very smart!' remarked Leon and, of course, they did share a love of History.

As well as being a keen student, Leon was also a member of the college's football team and one afternoon he tried to sell us tickets to the football club dance taking place that Friday night. Somehow Glenda and I felt obliged to buy tickets. On the night itself, I really didn't feel like going because I didn't particularly like dancing or crowds. I'd promised to meet Glenda and another friend outside the college's main court to go to the dance, but instead I just crawled into bed and started reading.

All of sudden, there was a forceful knock at the door. Unsurprisingly, it was Glenda, who'd come to get me. She literally dragged me out of bed, made me get dressed and forced me to go to the dance. When we got there, we were standing around and Leon came over. He looked even more dapper than the first time I'd seen him in his incredibly smart suit. My father Rice was a smart man, who got his suit fitted at the Co-op back in Tredegar, but Leon's suit was different: it looked sharper and it was clearly tailor-made.

In fact, there were three of us from Tredegar at that dance that evening: Glenda Williams, Ann Rogers and I. Leon, being a gentleman, danced with us all, and I was the last one he asked to dance.

'I'm sorry, I don't really dance very well,' I said.

'Oh, don't worry, just follow me. I'm a great dancer!' he smiled.

In fact, he wasn't. He was joking, but I just didn't realise it at the time. Then it came to a point in the dance where it was time for the interval.

'Great!' said Leon. 'You can buy me some refreshments.'

'I'm sorry, I don't have any money,' I blushed, feeling mortified. Once again, though, he was joking and, of course, he paid for the refreshments that consisted largely of sausage rolls. Once we'd got married, Leon loved nothing more than using that phrase – 'I don't have any money' – and adopting a Welsh accent in order to tease me. He even went so far as to retell that story to the assembled throng when Helen, our eldest daughter, got married in 1991, inserting it into his speech. Then again, as I found out quite quickly, Leon was capable of being both playful as well as incredibly serious, almost at the same time.

Leon was also naturally inquisitive. That night, as we finished up our coffees, he asked me why I didn't like dancing. I told him it was because my father had quite often forbidden me from going to dances back home.

'Do you want to go back to the dance, or do you want to go for a walk?' he asked.

In all honesty, I wanted to go back to the bed I'd just been dragged from and continue reading, but rather than say as much, I agreed to go for a walk with him. The college itself was off this long lane, so we strolled down there and continued chatting. Much later, again at assorted family gatherings, Leon would also retell the story of our meeting by saying, 'It all started in a country lane in Alsager …'

And I suppose it did, because that was the beginning of our life together. Well, almost …

* * *

'I can't see you this weekend,' said Leon as we walked back up the lane. The fact that we hadn't actually agreed to see each other appeared to have escaped him.

'Why not?' I asked all the same.

'Because I'm going to see Everton,' he explained.

'Who are they?' I asked.

It was at that point that I received an almighty shove for my troubles and almost ended up in a ditch! Then, after filling me in on the travails of the football team he supported, Leon informed me he was going back home that weekend.

'I'll see you in the lounge on Monday, though,' he added as we said goodnight.

When Glenda found out about our late-night stroll, she became slightly over-excited and spent most of the weekend gossiping about the situation, teasing me mercilessly. And, sure enough, that following Monday, after dinner, Leon strolled into the lounge and asked me if I wanted to go for another walk with him.

'Shall we go to the cinema in Crewe next Wednesday? I've got nothing else to do,' he added.

It might not have been the most romantic way of asking someone out, but I was delighted and as a result I agreed to go. And so, on that Wednesday, we caught the bus to Crewe and found a lovely café in which to eat. The food at college was terrible – 'Worse than army food!' snorted Leon – and I'd lost about eight pounds in weight in six weeks. I wasn't too bothered about my weight loss but my mother was, and she had begun to send me food parcels every few weeks to compensate for the college cuisine. I didn't really eat fried food, but on this occasion, I tucked into sausage and chips while Leon – the good Jewish boy that he was – ordered bacon, eggs and chips! Then we went to the pictures.

I can't honestly remember what film we saw but I do remember that we were both really conscious of the time because the college curfew was 10:30pm, and the walk back into the grounds took any potential latecomers past the principal's window. In retrospect, it's funny to think that Leon and some of the other male students who'd already been in the army would be happy to get in by 10:30pm, but I suppose these were different times. The pubs closed at 10pm in those days, and then there was nothing else to do. Equally, nobody wanted to challenge the principal's authority. Like I said, they were different days.

The college itself was located in a set of buildings that during the war had once been used to house the workers at the nearby Royal Ordnance Factory in Radney Green, which manufactured arms and ammunitions for the British Army. The buildings themselves were shaped like an 'H', with classrooms in two of the legs. The men's residence was at one end, the women's at the other – and never the twain were due to meet!

With Leon and I, it was obvious that we were attracted to each other, but it took a while for us to develop what I would call a boyfriend/girlfriend relationship. Looking back, I think everyone assumed that we were going out together before we did. In fact, there was lots of laughing at other couples because Leon found the concept of court-ship rather amusing in his own mischievous way.

Somehow or another he'd discovered that a lot of courting couples congregated by the mere in the town. On reflection, it was probably the only place they could go to escape prying eyes. One day, we went down there, and we became aware of all these couples on park benches, kiss-ing and in clinches. We started laughing quite loudly and in what must have seemed like quite a juvenile manner. Then, without further ado, Leon picked me up and started balancing me on a set of railings before threatening to drop me in the water – he found that particularly hilarious.

'See!' he shouted. 'No one else is doing this!' And, to be fair, they weren't. Instead, they were busy looking at us. But that was how our relationship was from the start. There was a lot of laughter, it was fun, and we really enjoyed each other's company.

In those early days, Leon used to say that I had big green eyes that he found attractive. When we were filming *Gogglebox*, there were also moments where he mentioned my legs – much to my dismay and embarrassment! But when we were at college, I think he also liked the fact that I dressed in quite a smart way. We were always supposed to dress for dinner. Women were discouraged from wearing trousers and men had to wear a jacket and a tie. Women were also expected to wear a blazer, skirt and heels – which sounds rather strange in this day and age, but it was all very formal, and usually the principal came in too, adding to the semi-pomp of the occasion. Thinking back, there was almost a touch of the public school about the ceremony of it all.

Anyhow, Leon was impressed with the fact that I wore straight skirts, offset with a smart top. The idea of being well turned out probably came from my mother, who was a dressmaker, and I was possibly at odds with other students. In those days, tartan was the 'in' thing, but I didn't have one scrap of it in my wardrobe, much to

Leon's delight. 'Trews', as Tartan trousers were known in those days, were a particular bugbear of his.

'I don't like those girls with big backsides and tartan trousers!' he used to say. I suppose people would find that quite outrageous now, but, as anyone who has seen him on television knows, he was capable of being very forthright, quite often in a manner that could be described as chauvinistic. In fact, nothing could've been further from the truth.

Leon also liked the fact that I didn't take things too seriously. As I got to know him, I appreciated his humour and I took him for who he was. At college, he was known as a joker and that was fine by me. He was also incredibly generous. Everywhere we went, he always paid. He had money, whereas I had a grant of something like £1 a week that I mainly spent on food. During his time in the army he'd actually saved some money, sent it home, and his mother had put it in a bank account for him. That was another major difference between us: he had a bank account while I still had a Post Office account.

He would never let me pay for anything and I began to find that embarrassing. Irritated, I consulted the oracle, Glenda, and she suggested that I should try and treat him to a meal, so I asked Leon if I could take him out. He looked at me as if I was slightly mad and simply wasn't having any of it. Then, one day, we were getting the bus somewhere to go for a night out and he reached into his pocket to get his wallet out, only to find he'd left it behind.

'I'm quite happy to pay,' I told him (and I was), but I could see he hated that. As we got to know each other, I noticed that he hated it when other people paid for things – it seemed to make him uncomfortable. That lasted for the whole of his life. He disliked meanness in people intensely, and enjoyed the act of giving.

When I think about it properly, I think Leon had this self-assurance that was very new to me. I was used to the lads back in Tredegar being quite brash. Some of them were rugby players, but a lot of them were very ordinary people who, like me, had fathers who worked in coal mining, steel works or building sites.

This guy had already been in the army – which made him different – but he could also talk about going to London, because he'd spent a lot of time there with his parents. In contrast, I had been to London for a day. He could also talk about going on holiday, whereas I had never been on a holiday in my life. My holidays involved staying with relatives in South Wales or going to Blackpool. He had already been abroad and travelled to Belgium, when London was as far as I'd got. All in all, he was a new type of person to me, but he was also very humble with it.

Leon had a sense of modesty that I found overwhelmingly charming. There was almost a shyness about him as well, which he did his level best to hide. It was only much later that I realised how seriously he took any kind of criticism, and maybe that was to do with his background and a desire to find a sense of belonging.

'Why are you so proud of being Welsh?' he'd ask me on various occasions.

'Because I come from Wales and my parents are Welsh,' I'd reply. In fact, when we were at college the very fact that I was Welsh became an issue when our PE teacher singled Glenda and I out and admonished us for having what she called 'a Celtic temperament'. I had always hated PE and I had no idea what she meant by that comment, but I did find it rather insulting. When I told Leon, he wanted to know whether I was bothered by it. I told him that I wasn't really, but that Glenda and I were different people so I didn't see why we would be banded together as if we were the same person just because we came from the same place. Of course, that kind of behaviour from a lecturer wouldn't be tolerated now. Leon completely understood how I felt about the situation and was completely supportive too.

I was proud of being Welsh, but Leon was hiding the fact that he was Jewish. He wouldn't even tell me at first. We had been going out for quite a long while when the subject finally came up. Leon had already been to Wales to meet my family, and both my mother and father had enjoyed his company tremendously, but I hadn't been to Ellesmere Port to meet his parents yet. He felt that this in itself was becoming a source of gossip among the other students.

'Have they been at you because I haven't taken you home?' he asked me apropos of no one in particular.

'No, they – whoever "they" are – have not,' I replied.

'I'm sorry, but I can't,' he said.

'Why not?'

'I just can't …' he winced. I was slightly puzzled by his apparent secrecy and unsure as to why he couldn't talk to me about whatever was worrying him.

In the end, it simply became clear that he could not bring himself to say 'because I am Jewish'. Later on, of course, he became immensely proud of his Jewish ancestry, but he was so uncomfortable about it all when we first met, possibly because he knew of the complications that arose when Jewish men married outside of the faith. It's only recently, now that he's gone, that I realise how much it troubled him back then.

'You were so happy as a child, weren't you?' he once remarked to me, and he was right, because I genuinely was. So was he, because his parents absolutely adored him, but for some reason, there was a shadow cast over him which took a long time to leave. It took him about 18 months to tell me about his faith.

At one point, our RE tutor – who was a confidante to a lot of the male students in college – took it upon himself to speak to me.

'I believe you're going out with Mr Bernicoff. You do realise he's Jewish, don't you?' he said.

I told him that I was fully aware of the fact and that it didn't make the blindest bit of difference to me. In all honesty, though, the cultural differences and our differing social backgrounds meant that in those early days, things weren't that straightforward between us. That said, I do think Leon felt he was on safe ground with me, and he had the sense that we should be together from a very early point in our relationship, even if he wasn't explicit about it.

Somebody we knew got engaged after six weeks of being in a relationship and I said to Leon: 'I'd be hauled over the coals if I did that. My father would go absolutely spare! I've got to make my way in the world before I even think of getting married.' And that was true. My father had worked hard all his life as a coal miner and he had always said to me that he didn't just want me settling down straight away. In those days, married women gave up work as soon as they'd tied the knot. My parents wanted something different for me. They wanted me to work, to make my own way, and to experience life for myself and become an independent woman. I appreciated that and I think Leon understood and admired that too.

I invited Leon to come home to Tredegar with me during the first summer holiday, in July 1956, and he accepted. While we discussed where we'd grown up, he told me that he lived above a gown shop that his parents owned. It was called Faye's, after his mother. Certain locals, however, called her 'Mrs Faye', thinking the 'Faye' family owned the shop due to the name. The shop itself was quite small and, often, as a shy teenager, he'd have to walk past women trying on clothes. This embarrassed him immensely and, over time, he'd come to hate the thought of it. I was quite surprised by this because by the time I met him, he had become very comfortable with women.

I had told my parents I had a boyfriend, and I told them his name. My father, who had always been very protective, liked Leon immediately when they met, the pair of them sharing an enthusiasm for sport. My brother Keith – who is seven years younger than me – was also strangely fascinated by him. I guess for those five days it was as if he had an older brother, rather than a bossy older sister!

That summer, I showed Leon around Tredegar, which I think he really loved, and we went to Cardiff and Swansea, and he met most of my friends. I have to confess that

I did keep him away from the rest of my extended family because I wasn't really sure where our relationship was heading, but we did have a great time together.

'He's a very nice boy,' said my dad once Leon had left. My mother was also charmed by him, most specifically because he adored the food she'd cooked him. To be honest, I assumed my family had realised during that first meeting that Leon was Jewish. In those days Tredegar was a town of just 22,000 people but it had its own synagogue and a sizeable Jewish community, members of whom they knew. But Leon's faith was never raised or referred to. Despite being protective of me, my parents were very liberal about things and they disliked any form of prejudice and made their views very clear on many occasions. Hence, I was quite surprised when later, as things got more serious between Leon and I, my parents made any kind of objection to the relationship. The truth was, though, that Leon and I were very different in so many ways.

CHAPTER 3

. . . .

June's Story

My earliest childhood memory is of me sleeping on the couch in the kitchen, which was the biggest room in our house. I can remember the warmth, the smells of my mother's cooking, the coal fire, and the distinct sense of security that came from just lying there. We lived in a small house on Ashvale, the road that gives its name to the area in which I grew up in Tredegar, South Wales. The terraced house we lived in was one of five and I was born there on 27th June 1937. It was a very close community, with other family members occupying the first and fifth houses on that terrace, while we lived in the third.

In those days, the backyards weren't enclosed and so, with all that open space, my mother, Blodwen, never quite knew where I was due to my propensity to wander off from an early age. From the age of three, I would go and get the bread at 11 o'clock every morning from the nearby bakery set up by my great-uncle Jack (then owned by his widow and family: Great Aunt Vi, Jinny and Jack, after his death – they were my second family as a child). It meant tackling a flight of heavy, steep stone steps, something my mother worried about tremendously.

'Don't worry,' I used to say, 'I can manage.'

In those pre-school days I would have a nap in the kitchen every afternoon, and I would wake up when my father, Rice, got home from work at about half past three. Then, he would wash his hands and have his dinner while still in his working clothes. He had bacon and eggs every day of the week. I'd sit with him while he ate, after which he'd get bathed and then take me out to play in the fresh air.

My father was five feet eight inches tall, slim, with dark hair and green eyes. In his working life he never exceeded ten stone. He worked in the local coal mine and every day, he'd catch the 5:40am train to travel one stop from the town to the pithead. The colliery itself was called Ty Trist – the name of which translates from Welsh into English as 'Sad House'. Thinking back, that really is an awful name. Some years after the mine closed, they built a comprehensive school on the site very close by and it seemed they intended to call it Ty Trist School. Thankfully, for fairly obvious reasons, they elected to name it Tredegar Comprehensive School instead.

At the time, I remember my father expressing his concern at the idea of building a school in such close proximity to the mine, for safety reasons. Of course, in 1966, there was the horrific disaster in Aberfan, another mining town that was only 10 miles away from where we lived, where the local school was buried under the slurry that slid down the hill, killing 116 children and 28 adults. The accident was related to the waste from the mine, rather than the mine itself, but it underlined just why my father had been concerned at the very thought of a school being located anywhere near the site of any former mining activity. When the Aberfan disaster happened, my younger brother Keith rushed to volunteer to try and find victims of the tragedy. He was an apprentice at the time and his boss lost two of his children on that terrible day – it was utterly heartbreaking.

Life in the pit was far from easy. My father worked incredibly hard to support our family because his was the sole source of income. My mother – a plump, attractive, fair-haired, blue-eyed woman, who was shy and slightly deaf too, but incredibly practical – had been a dressmaker and wonderful knitter. She gave up working once she got married, largely because my father felt that people didn't pay her enough. As a result, he made it clear that he would work overtime to make up the difference financially and ensure they had whatever they needed. That wasn't an uncommon situation in those days because most married women stopped work and tended to the home and family.

In fact, they also looked after the finances, as in those days the men 'tipped up' their pay at the end of the week – as the expression went. That meant that men would literally tip the money out of their pockets, and the women would sequester it away, giving their partners pocket money for beer and suchlike. Essentially, it also meant that women were like the chancellors of the exchequer of the home, controlling the budget and making sure there really was enough to get by.

My maternal grandmother, Jane, also played a large role in our lives. She owned our house and one in the next street she'd lived in. An interesting and enterprising woman, she'd been widowed at the age of 46. These days, mental health is openly talked about, but it wasn't back then. Her husband, Tom, had several issues that resulted in him taking his own life at the age of 48. But being widowed in such tragic circumstances didn't stop Jane from forging her own way in the world. She borrowed money from her brother – Jack, the baker, who lived next-door-but-one from us – to set up her own business when she was about 50, and bought clothing, material and bedding for people. She would take orders locally before travelling to Cardiff to buy what she needed from wholesalers. So successful was she that she made enough money to buy her first house outright, before buying a second.

By the time my brother Keith was born, seven years after me, my grandmother had come to live with us, because, at the age of 56, she'd had a stroke. She recovered slowly and, determined as ever, resumed her business with great support from my mother. This she continued to run even during the war and despite the obvious austerity inflicted by that time, the business continued to thrive.

World War II did change an awful lot of things for a lot of people. The Blitz, in particular, affected Cardiff terribly. I remember visiting the city on one occasion in 1942 with my grandmother. The previous day, a bomb had hit the area we were visiting and the smell was quite overpowering and hard to describe. On reflection, I was too young to realise the severity of it all, although I do remember everyone around me speaking in hushed tones as we walked through the damaged streets.

My early childhood, though, was different from a lot of those experienced by my friends, whose fathers were drafted into the army and went away to war. As a coal miner, my father was part of what they called a 'protected industry' and he had to keep on working because the war effort required coal. As well as working, he became our local ARP warden. That's probably not a job that people are familiar with these days, but the role of an Air Raid Precautions warden basically involved protecting civilians from German air raids and ensuring they took shelter in the appropriate manner. My uncle – who was my mother's brother, Noah – was also in the Home Guard, the local defence organisation. They used to practise their drills in front of our house and we'd sit on the wall and watch them, finding the whole thing hilarious – 'Halt! Who goes there?' was a line we loved repeating.

Of course, in the 1970s, the antics and endeavours of the Home Guard would form the basis for *Dad's Army*, the BBC TV comedy. As a result of that programme – and the excellent casting of the likes of Arthur Lowe as Captain Mainwaring, John Le Mesurier as Sergeant Wilson, Ian Lavender as Private Pike, and Bill Pertwee as ARP Warden Hodges – the Home Guard and ARP wardens became viewed as figures of fun, which was rather unfair. Thankfully, Father loved *Dad's Army*. So too did Leon, and the pair of them would often sit and watch it, with Leon laughing like a drain.

Much later, when Leon and I joined the cast of *Gogglebox*, we watched an episode of *Dad's Army* – the famous 'Don't tell them, Pike!' instalment, which is probably the most iconic moment in the programme's history. Looking back, I have to confess that I did think there were moments in that programme that were worryingly true to life.

* * *

From a very early age I loved school and learning about things. I attended Dukestown Primary School and my dad would pick me up from there every day. He'd get home from work, and then stroll through the fields, skip over what we called 'the river' – which was actually a small brook about a metre wide – and meet me outside the school, and we'd walk back home together. It was during one of those walks that he asked me what I wanted to do with my life.

'I want to be a teacher,' I said immediately. And from then onwards – bar a brief moment when I thought I wanted to be a nurse – my mind was genuinely made up. Teaching was really the thing for me from a very young age, probably because I had a number of inspirational teachers as a child.

The first was Miss Cosh – who became Mrs Atkinson – who lived a few doors away from us, and who developed my initial interest in reading. The second was Harry Evans, who had been away serving during the war, but returned in 1945 to teach us in our final two years at primary school. Having a male teacher at school was quite odd because at that point we'd only had female teachers due to the impact of military service, but he was inspirational.

Mr Evans taught us a lot about local history and he was very political. With him we studied the 1945 Election – a real turning point for the country, where Winston

Churchill's Conservatives were defeated by Clement Atlee's Labour Party. In order for us to understand what was going on, he organised a mock election for the class. Quite impressive, since we were only eight years old! But we did learn a lot from his rather practical approach.

As well as organising one of our first school trips, where he took us to Caerphilly Castle and then on to Barry Docks to see the ships coming in, Mr Evans was also instrumental in introducing us to poetry. In all honesty, we probably read a bunch of children's poets who are none too highly regarded now, but that wasn't the point: we were using our minds and discovering things that lay outside of our immediate, local environment. That was genuinely stimulating.

Another key influence during my early childhood was my best friend Glenda's mother, Agnes, who was a very intelligent, gifted lady. I can't remember a time when I didn't know Glenda. She lived about 200 yards away from me and we remained friends until she passed away at the age of 74 in 2011. Her mother was in a drama group in Tafarnaubach, a village about a mile away from Ashvale, and one evening, she asked us to come and help with a production the group was putting on.

Glenda and I were given the job of going to fetch any props that they were short of. There wasn't a local shop for these props or anything like that. Instead, we just had to visit various cast members' houses to grab the potential homemade props. At the time, we were only about seven and so, as night began to fall, we were like two little ants running through the village, bringing various things back to the hall where the performance was taking place. The nights in those days were pitch black because not only were there very few streetlights, but the wartime blackout was in full effect, meaning no lights were visible from the houses themselves. Thankfully, there was very little traffic on the road, so we were quite safe, but the whole thing did make us feel important. It was something so out of the ordinary and very exciting.

The play that the drama group were putting on was *Charley's Aunt*, the Brandon Thomas farce. Once we'd done all the fetching and carrying, as a reward we were allowed to sit on the hall floor and watch the play. I remember being utterly fascinated by it, not least of all because some of the cast featured men dressed as women! I went home and told my mother about that, and I was so excited by the whole thing she could barely get me off to sleep that night. There were three of these kinds of productions per year, and we absolutely loved them.

As well as the drama group, our local chapel also had a children's club known as A Band of Hope. It was quite formal, but they put on a pantomime every Christmas and, at the age of eight, I was asked to play a part in the chorus. That really was quite wonderful. We wore paper clothes and it was also the first time we were allowed to use make-up. That was totally new to me, and so thrilling!

I was ten years old when they opened a proper drama group in Tafarnaubach and I actually got to perform in my first play. I wish I could remember what it was! I was meant to be the understudy, but the girl who played the lead got a proper job so I had to step in. I was so nervous that I delivered my lines at about 100 miles per hour! But that was it: I was smitten with the theatre from then on. Unfortunately, I didn't continue acting when I transferred to Tredegar Grammar School because it was very competitive and I wanted to concentrate more on my studies. But my parents encouraged me to continue to go and see plays.

The local miners' association had an agreement with the Workmen's Hall, which meant that my father, as a member of the association, could get two tickets for the price of one. The hall put on two drama festivals per year, and Glenda and I were both able to go because of those cheap tickets. While the festival was on, it also meant that your homework was suspended, so we were doubly thrilled!

* * *

As well as the theatre, the other interest that my parents encouraged me to pursue was music. The music teacher hadn't really noticed me during my first year at secondary school until our exam results came in. It transpired that I'd actually done really well. So, as well as playing piano, I was given the opportunity to play the clarinet. My parents were very keen for me to do that, but I had to go to Cardiff for the lessons. That was 24 miles away, and it meant there was the fare to Cardiff as well as the fees for the lessons themselves that needed to be paid. There was also the cost of the clarinet itself. There was an arrangement that meant you were given a clarinet to use for a year, the hire of which would be paid for by the Local Education Authority. Once that year was over, though, if you were going to continue playing, you had to buy the clarinet outright. I was aware of the expense of all of this and felt it would be too much for my parents and so, despite their encouragement, I didn't take up the school's offer. Later on, though, my brother did, buying a clarinet and a saxophone when he was 16 and learning to play to quite a high standard.

Growing up in South Wales, we were surrounded by male voice choirs and when Leon came to Tredegar for the first time in the summer of 1956, I took him to watch a choir rehearse. He found it incredibly moving and powerful. I had also sung in an all-girl choir at school myself and appeared in a mixed production of Gilbert and Sullivan's *The Mikado* at the age of 14. In 1951, I'd also travelled to London for the first time to see *The Mikado* itself. It was a fantastic production that I really found enthralling.

In my youth, the power of music itself was really obvious to me because it was important to the families on both my mother and father's sides. Every Friday night, my father's family, the Edwards, would congregate at my paternal grandmother's house on the other side of town and play records. They would do so by sitting still and just listening to the music itself. Today, that probably sounds unusual, but music was not as ubiquitous as it is now – you had to make the effort to hear music, so they listened intently and genuinely lost themselves in what they heard. Of course, I was a child and therefore easily distracted, but all of the younger members of the family were told to sit quietly and listen, while the adults sat silently. During those intense moments, it actually seemed that we were transported to another world. In fact, I do remember, as I grew older, being overpowered by the emotion within the music they played and thinking I was going to cry because of the intensity of what I heard.

My father had a record collection that consisted mainly of classical music and he was very much into operatic arias. He knew the story behind every aria, even though he had never seen an opera. Then, when Beniamino Gigli, the celebrated Italian tenor, came to Cardiff, my father and his brothers went to see him. Tickets were £5 and that, as the saying goes, was 'a lot of money in those days'. They went by taxi and got caught in a snowstorm on the way back. In relative terms, it cost a fortune, but when my father eventually got home, he was just so thrilled by what he'd seen and incredibly animated.

It wasn't until I was in the sixth form that I was allowed to go and see my first opera as part of a school trip. We were offered the opportunity to go and see *Nabucco*, written by the Italian composer Giuseppe Verdi. I went home with the letter, detailing the trip and the cost of it, and my father couldn't sign it quickly enough. He put his hand in his pocket and gave me the money straight away. I went to see it and was absolutely enthralled. The trip home from Cardiff was quite long and I got back after midnight. My father – who was both incredibly supportive to me as well as very protective – was still waiting up and, even though he had to be up before five o'clock in the morning, he wouldn't go to sleep until I'd exhausted him with every last detail of exactly what I'd seen.

My father was also a fan of Paul Robeson, the American singer, actor and activist, who had an amazingly deep voice, and who had visited Wales in the late 1920s and developed an affinity with the mining communities in particular. A confirmed socialist, by the '50s, Robeson had been blacklisted in the US during the McCarthy era due to his political beliefs. My father had missed seeing him during his first trips to Wales. Then, years later, Robeson appeared at the National Eisteddfod – a week-long cele-bration of Welsh culture – in Ebbw Vale, which is the next town to Tredegar, and we all went to hear him. By that point, I was 18 and Robeson's voice was possibly starting to go, but he was still able to sing so low, it was incredible and, of course, I was old enough to really be able to appre-ciate him. In fact, thinking back to that time, I realise now that I have always been attracted by certain voices. Even Leon's, which, believe it or not, was seductively deep and mysterious when I first met him.

I think it was that sense of mystery that attracted me to things when I was younger. In the days before televi-sion, music and drama were great sources of mystery and escapism. So too, of course, were books. At school, we didn't do much in the way of modern literature but I do remember being captivated by descriptive writing, espe-cially the works of Thomas Hardy, the Victorian realist, whose attention to detail was mesmerising, even if the subject matter was sometimes rather bleak.

On a lighter note, when I was at secondary school, I also remember that there was a huge fuss about *Lady*

Chatterley's Lover, the novel by D.H. Lawrence. It had been deemed pornographic and immoral. As schoolkids, we had no real idea what that meant, but we'd studied Lawrence's other novels, so we felt obliged to ask our teacher about *Lady Chatterley*. He knew straight away that we weren't likely to let the matter drop so he attempted to diffuse the situation.

'If you want to read that book that badly then I will sign your library tickets so that you can borrow it,' he announced with a smile. For a split second, we were euphoric. Then, the realisation dawned on us that we would have to follow through with this. In fact, I don't think any of us did because we were simply too worried about being caught with a copy of the book by our parents.

In the end, I'd already become a teacher myself before I finally got around to reading *Lady Chatterley's Lover*, and I think I may be one of the few pupils from Tredegar Grammar School who actually did read it! In 1960, the book became the subject of an obscenity trial, its publishers Penguin Books being pursued under the Obscene Publications Act due to the colourful language contained in the text. Following a six-day trial, a verdict of 'not guity' was delivered. Ironically, there are far more graphic books you can read these days. That whole episode, though, was indicative of the naivety associated with our teenage years and the fact that all children at that age possess the power to embarrass their teachers and their elders. Thankfully, that is still the case today – long may it continue!

* * *

One of the most significant moments during the course of my secondary education involved one particular prize-giving ceremony during my first year at Tredegar Grammar School. As with most schools, it was an annual event, with prizes awarded to the Upper and Lower Schools. My ambition was to win a prize for English so I could go to Stratford and see one of Shakespeare's plays performed in his birthplace. Unbeknownst to me, however, they'd changed the prize from a rather exciting trip, and commuted it to a plain old English dictionary. So, while I was thrilled to actually win the prize, the outcome was somewhat deflating.

As was the case every year, the big prize that was awarded was the Aneurin Bevan Prize for Languages. The prize itself consisted of £40 awarded to the best language student in order to allow them to travel to France and experience that culture first-hand. Nye Bevan – as everyone called him – was our local Labour MP. He had been born in Tredegar in 1897 and, just like me, he had a coal miner for a father and a seamstress mother. He had gone to work at the Ty Trist colliery before becoming a union representative and moving into politics. A big man with a big voice, at that point he was possibly the nearest equivalent that Tredegar had to a local celebrity – although describing him as such possibly does him a disservice.

When he turned up to address the Upper School, he didn't talk to us about languages or any such sort. Instead, he just talked about the importance of education. For the boys, he said, education was a way out of the mines, the quarries and the steelworks. Horrific accidents often happened in all three of these industries. 'Things in those industries are often paid for by men's lives,' he said. 'And what about the girls?' he asked rhetorically, in that remarkably rich voice. 'We don't want our girls going up to London to service anymore! We know what happens to our girls that go up there. They have to scrub and scrape, and worse things happen to them!' he thundered.

He talked to us about the option of going on to university, which very few people had done at that time, and going into teaching too. But above all of that, he pointed out that women would be the principal educators of our own families. A mother, he said, was the person who instilled real values in the family, and a real sense of education. As a result, women had the power to change society itself as well as having an impact on our local culture. It was a remarkable, empowering speech made more so by the fact that Bevan came from exactly the same background as all of us, yet he had managed to escape the mines.

He talked about how he had won a scholarship to a college in London, and how he had become an MP. That, he said, also meant that he had the power to change things, which, of course, he was doing in a very literal sense. We had already learnt all about the landslide victory that the Labour Party enjoyed at the 1945 election and we knew that Bevan was in the Cabinet, where he had been appointed minister of health. In fact, he was instrumental in establishing the National Health Service, which was based on the premise that good healthcare should be available to everyone, and at no cost.

In fact, the principles behind the NHS were already long established in Tredegar because we had a system called Medical Aid Society, which had been set up by the Miners' Association in the 1930s. Every miner paid thruppence (threepence) in the pound to a fund, and that fund was used to provide healthcare. My father had signed up to this and it meant that he and his dependents had access to all sorts of services. In very practical and personal terms, I'd already had my tonsils removed under this scheme!

Bevan's vision was one that has continued to endure, and his speech at my school on that day came over very loud and clear. He obviously wanted to give us hope for the future. But beyond that, he wanted to make us understand that individuals really *did* have the power to change things, regardless of class or creed.

As well as instituting the NHS, Nye Bevan also had this vision where he wanted every family to live in a house with a garden. He believed that a sense of security would instil a sense of pride and remove a lot of the problems that society was facing back then. It's ironic, thinking about it now, at a time when housing is still a real issue. Of course, Bevan was a man of action as well as a fantastic idealist, but his idealism was based in optimism, and that was most definitely a viewpoint Leon and I shared, even though we came from completely different backgrounds. In a number of respects, it would be easy for Leon to have been a right-wing Tory. In fact, he was the complete opposite and, as *Gogglebox* viewers will know only too well, pretty vocal with it too!

CHAPTER 4

. . . .

Leon's Story

I think that Leon would probably be the first to admit – reluctantly, of course – that he was indulged as a child. He would probably say that being the only child in a Jewish family made it unavoidable. That's possibly true and it helps to explain just how and why his parents, Maurice and Faye, doted on him during his younger years.

Leon's family history is quite complicated. At first, we thought that his mother's family originated from Poland, but, as we loosely traced his family tree, we found out eventually that both his parents' families had actually escaped from Russia during the pogroms of the early 1900s during which the Jewish people were persecuted there. His mother's parents had settled in Hanley, Staffordshire, and his father's family had made their home in Liverpool, which is where Leon was born on 27th October 1934. His parents moved to Ellesmere Port, Cheshire, in 1932, and there they opened a shop selling women's clothes, Faye's.

Initially, though, Leon's dad Maurice had been quite musical and he'd played violin in Billy Cotton's jazz band, one of the most popular acts of that time, for two weeks, filling in for another musician. As a teenager, he was also offered a job playing on one of the liners that sailed out of Liverpool, but his parents wouldn't let him go. Had Maurice pursued music, there's every chance that Leon's life would have been completely different. That said, one inescapable truth would undoubtedly have remained: Leon was gloriously tone-deaf, as anyone who heard him sing in assembly would be able to attest.

Growing up in Ellesmere Port in the 1930s was tough for a young Jewish child, with anti-semitism increasingly on the rise as the decade progressed. The Bernicoffs also happened to be the only Jewish family in the area, and the only family with their name in the whole of the UK. When war finally broke out, Maurice was drafted into the army and went off to fight. His father's absence added to Leon's increasing sense of insecurity. With Maurice away, Faye's sister, Bessie, moved in, with her husband Izzy, their son Harold, and their daughter Shirley, who had Down's syndrome. Six months older than Leon, she became almost like a sister to him at that point. He would tease her unmercifully before becoming incredibly protective of her, something which lasted into later life.

In many respects, Leon grew up in a very female-oriented household during those early, formative years, with the shop's manageress, Miss Evan, contributing further to that. Growing up with so many women around him meant that he was always very relaxed in female company in later life. Some of the things he said when we filmed *Gogglebox* may have been interpreted as chauvinistic, but in fact he was also very supportive of women throughout his entire life. That said, he did also learn how to wind them up from an early age and, just as significantly, he learnt how to get his own way almost all of the time!

Maurice had joined the Royal Artillery Corps and was a driver and a plotter – the person who marks out positions on a map. He was part of General Montgomery's Eighth Army (also known as The Desert Rats) and lived through a lot of remarkable experiences during that time, all of which we later found out about. The stories of his time in the army seemed quite extraordinary. On one occasion, for instance, Monty was visiting his troops when they started shouting at him. 'When will we go home?' yelled one. 'You'll fight your bloody way back!' was the General's uncompromising response.

In the summer of 1943, Maurice was on a landing craft going into Sicily, but they couldn't get the craft close enough so they all had to wade to the shore. Maurice was only five feet three tall – or five feet three and three-eighths, as he used to be fond of pointing out – and the water went straight over his head as he disembarked. Then, when he landed, he was shot in the leg. In later life, he loved to show everybody his scars, but at the time, things were a little more serious. Lying on the beach, wounded, he really thought he was going to die.

A Roman Catholic priest turned to him and said, 'We will take care of you, my son. And we will make sure you get home.' Apparently, a member of the Salvation Army sat with him and he dictated a letter home to say he was safe. Before his letter could arrive, though, Leon's mother received a telegram from the War Office stating her husband was 'missing, presumed dead'. She was obviously totally distraught and preparing Leon for the fact that he might never see his father again when the second letter from Maurice arrived.

Around the same time as that was happening to Leon's family, I was still in Tredegar. I remember running into Glenda's mother on the bus, who showed my mother and I a similar telegram she'd received, saying her husband was also 'missing'. He was a paratrooper and he'd been shot down at the Battle of Arnhem in Holland. In fact, they subsequently found out that he was a prisoner of war (POW) and he returned home after the war. Essentially, it seems the chaos of war caused this level of misinformation to occur on quite a regular basis, and it was incredibly distressing.

Faye was obviously relieved when she found out that Maurice was still alive. Originally, it seemed as though he was to be invalided out of the army, but that didn't happen in the end. Instead, he went back and fought some more, moving on to Palestine and the area that soon became Israel. When Maurice finally came home in 1945, Leon was nine and he didn't know him and so, as his father walked through the door, Leon ran and hid behind his mother. It took a while for him to emerge from there to greet his father properly. Subsequently, he was hugely embarrassed by the whole situation and, even in later life, he would say that when he thought about that incident, he could still feel his cheeks turning red.

His father had been away for five years and during that time Leon had grown up quite considerably. Maurice endeared himself instantly to his son by bringing him home a proper leather-cased football, meaning that Leon was the only child in his neighbourhood to possess such a prized item. Eventually, the pair got to know each other again and Leon would also take great pride in parading around the house wearing his father's helmet. He used to talk about carrying his father's rifle around too, but I'm not entirely sure that soldiers were allowed to take their firearms home after the war. Of course, it could have been another of Leon's great exaggerations, of which there were quite a few down the years!

I don't think Leon was consciously affected by his father's absence initially, but I think when he reflected on that time he realised that he had missed having a male role model around during those early years. His uncle Izzy had taken him to his first Everton game, but that wasn't quite the same thing. His father's absence also meant that his mother was incredibly protective of Leon. Equally, when Maurice came home, he tried to make up for lost time by spoiling his son rotten. This endless amount of attention meant that Leon also learnt to play his parents off against each other, at times with quite spectacular results!

On one occasion, his mother bought him a beige raincoat. However, Leon wanted one that was navy, like everybody else. As a result, he threw something of a tantrum in the Bon Marché department store in Liverpool. He stormed off, but Maurice took Leon to a cinema called News Theatre (as it was known in those days) for a cooling-off period in an attempt to diffuse the situation. Knowing how much his son wanted a navy raincoat, though, Maurice went back to the store to buy it for him. In the end it meant that Leon not only got what he wanted, but ended up with two raincoats. Clothes were also an important part of the Bernicoffs' life as far as their business was concerned.

Prior to the war, Maurice had worked on various markets, running clothing stalls, spending time in places as far afield as London's Petticoat Lane, on occasion. When he was discharged from the army, he and Faye decided that she would continue to run the shop while he would return to running the stall, so they would have two incomes. Warrington Market was the most lucrative of those markets, and Maurice did a roaring trade there. He also enjoyed market life and worked Wednesdays, Fridays and Saturdays well into his sixties.

Much later, when Leon and I were together, we used to go and visit him there and we loved the bustle of it all. On one occasion, Maurice had the misfortune of leaving Leon in charge of his stall, but Leon just wandered off and started talking to someone he knew. All of a sudden there was an almighty commotion and this voice screaming: 'Leon!!!! You've lost me a customer by not paying attention!' Leon just gave his dad the 'Leon smile' and I think it was quite clear at that point that he had very little business sense and was unlikely to follow in his father's footsteps.

* * *

There was an evening not too long before Leon died when he was reflecting on his childhood: 'Nobody fully understands racism unless they have experienced it.' This was a comment he had made many, many times over the years, but had never enlarged upon it. But that night, he recalled that as a child, comments were made about his funny name, the fact that he was a Jewish boy with curly hair, or, more precisely, 'the Jew boy who lived over the shop'.

'I just longed to be plain John Smith who lived in a house like everyone else,' he added. To a boy who came from the only Jewish family in Ellesmere Port these comments – although not directed at him that often – clearly had a lasting effect and still hurt him very deeply down the years.

Leon was a very bright, intelligent child and did extremely well at Whitby Heath Primary School, where he came joint top of his year. He always spoke with great respect and affection of his teachers there, who gave him such encouragement. His mother wrote to his father, telling him of Leon's achievement. Maurice – who was still serving in the army at that point – insisted she send Leon to The King's School in Chester as he wanted him to have the opportunities he himself had never had. So, at eight years old, Leon changed schools. Every day he caught the 8am bus to Chester. He was to remain at The King's School

– which was not a fee-paying school at the time – until he was 18. Some years later, his best friend, Bob O'Callaghan, transferred to Chester City Grammar School and was to join Leon on that bus journey. Who knows what they got up to during their trips to and from school? Somehow, they always seemed to find some sort of mischief!

Bob was two years younger than Leon and they lived a few doors down from each other. They stayed friends right through school and even when they both went into the army at different times. In a way, they were like brothers. Leon told me that as kids they often wrestled in the drawing room over his parents' shop, causing a terrible racket. Leon's father would storm up the stairs to tell them off. They would hear him coming, so he would emerge to find them red-faced, sweating, but holding a hand of cards each as if nothing else had happened.

As they reached their teens, Leon and Bob started going dancing and getting girlfriends. By the time I got to meet Bob, he and Leon would obviously go out drinking. Bob was taller than Leon, with fair hair and blue eyes, and shared Leon's sense of humour. The two of them were known locally as 'Berni' and 'Cal', and they had developed quite a reputation with the ladies. They both loved this pub, where there was a piano, and they'd sing along with whoever was playing. Leon always used to say they were rather like Chas & Dave, which, bearing in mind his total lack of musical ability, is quite hard to believe! But they really were thick as thieves. At one point, Leon managed to get himself barred from the local library – he hadn't been talking, he'd just been pushing books off the top shelf. Once Leon was barred, Bob walked out in protest as a show of solidarity.

Initially, Leon did quite well at his new school and he received a bursary that allowed him to stay on through secondary school. Maurice realised at that point that his son was quite bright and, like most parents, he really wanted to provide him with the opportunities he himself had never had. He had high hopes for Leon, but then sport intervened. Leon played football and then he got into the first cricket XI at 14 – making him one of the youngest players in the team. He admitted that during the Easter holidays, he was just out at the nets all the time when, really, he should have been revising for exams. Academically, Leon didn't do as well as he could have. Added to that was his inbuilt sense of mischief. In fact, he used to say that during his time in the sixth form his father was in school as much as he was! That's how much trouble he used to get into.

In secondary school, his History teacher, Mr Yates, had a tremendous influence on him and, as a result, he became heavily interested in Politics and Social History. Those subjects sparked a will to learn that stayed with him for the rest of his life. His A-levels were far from a success, but Hull University offered him a place to read History. He elected not to go.

'I got a better invitation!' he used to say. 'An invitation from The Queen!'

By that, he meant that he'd joined the army because National Service was still compulsory in those days. Like his father, Leon served in the Royal Artillery for two years. He didn't enjoy the first few weeks of training which, like those endless army-based comedy films, appeared to involve him struggling to get over walls and falling into pools of water.

His parents attended his passing-out parade and the officer in charge came over to them and said: 'They turn up here as boys and we make men of them!' Apparently, Faye shot him a withering look and promptly replied: 'Actually, he was very nice beforehand and quite grown-up, thank you very much!'

During his time in the army, Leon was stationed to the east of London and he used his time there to explore the city at night. He knew the centre of town quite well because his parents had taken him to London from an early age, and this time around, he went to various clubs only to get back to his barracks at an ungodly hour. On one occasion, he was so late he found himself facing a charge, but he was so well-liked by his fellow cadets that everybody clubbed in; they provided him with the necessary bits of fully-shined kit and helped him prepare for inspection to ensure he didn't get into any further trouble.

On a more sombre note, he became a clerk in the army and learnt to type as a result. He also claims that it was during that time that he was approached by MI5 and asked to attend an interview. I'm not sure anyone ever actually believed that story. After all, it did seem rather unlikely!

'Why would they choose you?' I used to say. 'Bernicoff isn't exactly a discreet name and you can't keep a secret to save your life!' Leon, of course, swore it was true. Meanwhile, the rest of us found it hard to picture him in a James Bond-style role!

CHAPTER 5

The Perils of Courting

By June 1956, Leon and I had been going out for about 10 months. One afternoon, we went for tea at Little Moreton Hall in Cheshire, which is now owned by the National Trust. We cycled there, but along the way, Leon clumsily hit my front wheel with his bike, so I ended up falling on to the road! We dusted ourselves down and ended up having a lovely time in this rather posh manor house. It was then that Leon told me he wanted to take me down to London for my 19th birthday. That just seemed incredibly exciting.

My parents came up to Alsager that Sunday to surprise me and that was when they first met Leon. They were very impressed because he was in his cricket whites, and he was wearing his King's School blazer and a cravat. In fact, he always refused to wear the college blazer and despite everything that he said about public schools during our time on *Gogglebox*, he was incredibly proud of the fact that he'd been to King's School. During that visit, my father gave me £5 as a birthday gift and I decided to spend it during our big trip to the big city. To be honest, I gave Leon the money to look after because I was petrified that I'd get pickpocketed.

The day of our departure I met him by the college gate at five o'clock in the morning and then we eventually got to the main road, where we could hitch-hike to London. This beautiful car pulled up and Leon kindly put me in the back and gave me a cushion so I could get some sleep. The man who gave us a lift was a member of Her Majesty's Inspectorate of Education, a teaching inspector. While I snoozed on the back seat, Leon sat in the passenger seat and, for the best part of our three-and-a-half-hour drive, proceeded to tell this poor man just how *he* thought the education system should be run! He dropped us at Baker Street station and was probably relieved to see the back of us – although he did give Leon his card and suggest he ring him once he'd qualified, if ever he needed a job.

We travelled down to Piccadilly tube station and Leon decided he needed to visit the gents' and told me to wait for him up at street level. I went up there on my own and found the whole experience terrifying. The noise! The people! The lights! It was just so busy. I had never seen anything like it before. Leon, of course, was simply used to it and he really knew his way around the West End.

We'd booked a hotel near Warren Street – separate rooms, of course, because things between us were very innocent in those days – so we made our way up there and checked in. Then, we met one of Leon's army friends, who took us for a drink and gave us two tickets to *The Pajama Game*, the musical that had opened a year before at the London Coliseum. I was thrilled because it meant going to the theatre. In London! It was a wonderful treat.

The next day, Leon took me on a tour of the different parts of London that he knew. We walked down Fleet Street, up to St Paul's, and then back towards Downing Street and Westminster Abbey. We also went to Hyde Park Corner, and Donald Soper – the famous clergyman, socialist and preacher – was actually there on his soapbox! I didn't realise they used real soapboxes to preach from, so that was a revelation. Then I had my photo taken by the Serpentine, and Leon said, 'We'll come back on Christmas Day and have a swim!' Thankfully, we never did.

Eventually, we went back to Euston and got the train home, but those two days in London just confirmed what I'd known previously: Leon really was a man of the world, and he had so much more experience in life than I had. And I was impressed by that.

* * *

The following year, in June 1957, once our final exams were over, Leon and I were able to go on our last college trip together. I was thrilled that we were heading to Snowdon, the highest mountain in Wales. As always on these trips, we set off at the crack of dawn and spent several hours on the coach. It was a very pleasant day when we arrived at the foot of the mountain, and we prepared ourselves for the climb. Leon was in high spirits and decided I should give him a piggyback. How juvenile!

After an initial bout of larking around, we began our ascent properly. Everything seemed to be going rather well until the moment when we'd almost reached the summit. Suddenly, the weather changed, and quite dramatically, a heavy mist descended. The chatter stopped; it was time to concentrate on the walk. Suddenly, I slipped off the path and started to slide down the mountainside. Then, I stopped and managed to cling to a piece of rock. Terrified to move or make a sound, all I could hear was Leon's booming voice, followed by my tutor's more reasoned one, telling me to keep very still and to stay calm.

A few minutes later, the teacher reached me. I was shaking, and after much persuasion, I gave him my free hand. He told me to look up, and then I saw another student was leaning over the ledge and holding out his hand to grab my other wrist and help winch me up. I say 'winch' because that's how it felt. It was only when I got back on to the path that I realised I'd only really slipped a few feet. Had I not been so frightened, I could possibly have made my own way back on to the path. Leon looked relieved. He hugged me and took my arm to lead me to the summit. We were there in a matter of minutes.

'The lengths some people go to, to get a cup of hot tea!' laughed our tutor, handing me a hot sweet mug of tea from his flask by means of comfort. We sat at the top of the mountain, me in floods of tears and Leon white-faced. He held me tight as I continued to shiver from the shock of what had just happened. Not long afterwards, we began our descent. Of course, the mist gradually lifted and we were able to admire the beautiful scenery. I felt slightly foolish. Just as my drama subsided, another student fell and broke his leg. This time it was serious and Mountain Rescue had to be called, bringing our escapade to a sobering end.

We had booked a group meal in Bangor to celebrate the end of our trip and the end of our exams. By the time we got there, it was so late that the restaurant was closing, the food itself having been ruined. Our disappointment was acute. Leon wandered off for a few minutes and returned, beaming.

'I've found a chip shop!' he announced with glee. Of course, he was instantly proclaimed the hero of the hour! And I felt a certain pride in that.

July marked the end of our course at Alsager and our parents were invited to Open Day. Leon's parents drove from Ellesmere Port and, since my parents didn't have a car, my aunt Maud and uncle Johnny drove my parents up from South Wales. My parents and I enjoyed the day immensely, seeing the students' work and meeting the people I'd spent the last two years with.

As they were about to leave, we literally bumped into Leon and his mother and father. Leon had never hidden our relationship from his parents, but a moment's awkward silence was followed by introductions and polite conversation about the various displays of work we'd all seen, as well as our time at college. The conversation turned to the fact that college life was coming to an end, and we would soon have to venture into the real world. Then, after a short while, both families took their leave and walked in opposite directions. It was obvious neither set of parents was completely happy with our relationship. Leon and I could sense that, but we really did not know what we could possibly do about it.

* * *

That September, I started work at Butler Street Junior School and I threw myself into teaching. I loved it at first because I had a fantastic deputy head, who really looked after me, but sadly he died at the end of the first month. I really didn't enjoy the school quite as much after that, largely because the headmistress was a bit of a dragon. Butler Street had been amalgamated into a school for boys and girls. I was quite comfortable with this because I'd gone to a mixed school, but not everybody was. I gravitated to what had once been the former men's staffroom and I think the head disapproved of that and generally viewed me as an awful girl from South Wales. Regardless, I got through my probationary year.

Meanwhile, things between Leon and I were much the same as they had been at Alsager, although we did split up for a while. I had been home for Christmas and I had had a lovely time being spoilt by my family, enjoying my mother's cooking and the round of festive family parties and get-togethers, which I loved. However, I had come back alone to Liverpool as Glenda was ill. After a long and tedious journey which involved waiting around for endless train connections, I finally arrived at Lime Street Station hoping to see Leon. Alas, he wasn't there. I knew he was playing football for his new club, Haroldeans, that Sunday (I guessed the team were out together) so I took the bus back to the flat Glenda and I shared. It was cold, dismal and felt damp. I made something to eat and, feeling rather sorry for myself, went to bed.

Later that week, Leon and I met up and he talked enthusiastically about school, Everton and his new football team. In contrast, I felt I had nothing positive to contribute to the conversation. In fact, by the end of the evening, things had taken a distinct turn for the worst and we had essentially decided to split up. It seemed things had really changed as 1958 was upon us: here I was in a job I wasn't enjoying, living in a flat that was miserable and costing me a fortune, and now I had no Leon.

I wrote home to break the news to my parents. By return post came a letter from my mother who had been appointed as the family's chief scribe many years ago. She wrote that she thought the split was for the best as, although she and my father liked Leon very much, they both thought there was no possibility of a future for us together. This, it was clear, was due to our different faiths.

Glenda was back by the time I received that letter and, as ever, she allowed me to talk things through and offered wise words. Between us we decided that, despite the emotional upset of it all, our main priority was to find somewhere else to live. We were lucky enough to be able to move to Thingwall Residential School (of which more later, dear reader!)

I didn't see Leon for about three weeks, then one day I got a phone call from him at school, asking me whether I would meet him straight from school the next day.

I talked it over with Glenda. 'It's up to you now, whether you actually want to see him at all,' she told me. I decided that I did want to.

During the course of that evening Leon explained that his parents had also said that they too saw no future for us together. Well, at least it meant that both sets of parents agreed! We both talked openly and by the end of the evening, after something of a shaky start, we were laughing and joking about our predicament. Above all, though, we were really enjoying being together again. It was at that point that Leon made a rather confident promise: things would change.

* * *

The fact that I no longer had to pay rent meant for the first time in my life, I had money that I could spend on myself. My parents also had an agreement with me that involved them giving me a lump sum of money on the understanding that during the course of the year, I would save enough of my income to have doubled that original sum. I think they were just trying to teach me the value of saving money, but looking back, it was also quite a sacrifice on their part because it wasn't as though we were rich in the first place.

Since we were enjoying ourselves so much, Glenda and I decided to go on holiday together, and visit the World's

Fair in Brussels. Also known as Expo 58, it was basically a huge international exhibition, where different countries showed off the most advanced products that they had developed. Trade and international relations were celebrated, and cultural exchanges encouraged. In fact, it all seemed very *modern*.

We decided we'd go on holiday for a week and that cost us just under £20 (£19, 19s and 11 pence, if you *must* know!). Of course, we needed a passport to travel across the Channel, but you had to be 21 to get one yourself, and when we booked the trip, we were still technically under-age so we needed our parents' consent to get the necessary forms filled in. It was quite odd when you consider that Glenda and I were deemed responsible enough to look after 40 children, day and night, but we were still considered too young to vote and apply for our own passports.

We eventually got our passports and that summer we left Liverpool and headed down to London by coach. It was a boiling-hot day and when we stopped in Cheltenham en route, Glenda went to get us a lemonade to cool us down. Sadly, they didn't have any, so she got us two lagers instead. I took one sip and hated it, but Glenda drank most of hers as we carried on the journey on that overheated coach. As soon as we got in to Victoria coach station, she was violently sick in a bin. I was laughing madly about this, much to Glenda's irritation and general upset. To be fair, I don't think it was the one lager that made her ill. In the end we blamed the sheer heat of the coach. I'm not sure what passers-by thought, though, because the sight of two girls travelling together would have been viewed as quite odd in those days, let alone the fact that one of them had her head in a bin! Either way, we were quite oblivious to any kind of reaction and were just excited about what seemed like a wild adventure to us both.

We planned to go into the centre of town to see what was going on, but once we'd arrived in London, we felt a lot less bold. Despite the fact that I'd already visited the city with Leon, I still didn't know my way around and we both felt terrified about getting lost. As a result, that evening was spent doing little more than walking the streets near our hotel, literally around the block in a sort of square. The next day, we headed to Dover, and got on a ferry so crowded it felt like we'd arrived at a cattle market. We could only see about six lifeboats hanging up on the ferry too. I turned and said to Glenda, 'If this ship goes down, we're all going to drown!' That made us feel even more worried.

When we eventually got to Ostend, we met our holiday rep, who took us to our hotel and told us to wait to one side. For a minute we thought the hotel didn't have a room for us, but as it turned out, they'd upgraded us to a fantastic room in the main building. 'I'll be back tonight at dinner to collect the money for your trip to the World Fair,' our rep told us. The hotel manager overheard this and as soon as we were alone, he told us that we could get to Brussels for far less than we were being charged. That was remarkably kind of him. So, the next morning, we avoided the rep and decided to head off to Brussels on our own, armed with sandwiches and water that the hotel had kindly given us.

We got to Brussels and saw the *Manneken Pis* – the world-famous statue of the naked boy urinating into the fountain – and, as everyone who has ever visited the city will understand, we found it utterly hilarious. And, of course, we had to buy a postcard of the statue for the sake of posterity. Then, we got the free shuttlebus to the fair itself and what we saw there was amazing.

The centrepiece of the World's Fair was this building called The Atomium, which looked like a gigantic collection of interconnecting atoms linked by a series of walkways. It cost 50 pence to visit and that seemed rather expensive, so instead we spent our time visiting the British and American exhibits at the fair.

Glenda was keen to visit Holland because her father had been shot down there during the war, so we took advantage of a day trip to Middelburg, a city in the south-west of the country. He'd been taken in by the Dutch Resistance before being captured by the Germans, and he was held in a prisoner of war camp for nine months before it was liberated at the end of the War. We arrived in the city and walked into a bar and these men started to speak to us. I told them that Glenda's father had fought in the war and that he'd been captured at Arnhem. The next thing we knew, food and more drink started to arrive as if by some kind of thank you. Everyone wanted to know about the experiences that Glenda's father had been through and it was almost as if she'd become an instant local celebrity! I was very happy to ride on her coat-tails too, during the course of what was a rather fantastic afternoon.

When we got back to Tredegar, we were rather exhausted by our escapades, but we went straight back to work in September. Thingwall Special School housed children at the time described as 'educationally sub-normal'. It seems unbelievable now that the pupils could be referred to in this way because it's such a horrible description, but they were – the school itself was known as an ESN school. We had girls mainly from Liverpool, but also from as far afield as Birmingham. Working with them could be quite tough and emotionally demanding. It was the kind of work that made us grow up quite quickly, but so too had the experience of travel. The whole trip made me decide that I wanted to be more independent and do more things. Glenda felt the same, although later that year, she met Ken, the man who would become her husband.

Christmas was quite hard that year because we'd had an outbreak of chickenpox at Thingwall and the school was open during the festive period, which meant we were required to work for part of it. Although we went home for Christmas itself, we were only there for about four days and then we had to come back and resume our duties until the new term began again. It was challenging looking after children from other residential special schools who were sent to Thingwall over the Christmas period, some of whom found it very hard to acclimatise. Nonetheless, looking after the children was rewarding and we also learnt certain practical skills, one of which involved managing a daily budget.

Glenda and I were also due to start new jobs in January in special day schools – establishments which today would be known as schools for children with moderate learning difficulties rather than special needs schools. While we would both continue to live at Thingwall and work there in the evenings, we were both looking forward to our new jobs, although neither of us had anticipated the extreme weather which greeted our change in employment. In late January 1959, a blanket of thick and seemingly immovable fog descended over the Merseyside area to the point where you literally could not see your own hand in front of your face. We had never experienced anything of this kind in South Wales. Ice and snow, yes. Fog that caused such chaos, no. On two or three occasions we had to walk the three miles home from our separate day schools as all the buses in the city were cancelled.

Our new job was taxing but satisfying, meaning that our weekends were precious. We used to look forward to them tremendously. One Sunday I got a call from Leon telling me he was unable to make the trip from his parents' house in Ellesmere Port to Liverpool for our appointed rendezvous, so I was less than impressed. The fact that the fog – or smog as it may well have been – had descended and once again forced the cancellation of all public transport was neither here nor there. Common sense most definitely did not prevail. Instead, my acute disappointment did. It also manifested itself in extreme annoyance. I suggested that Leon drive over instead – something which in retrospect was rather stupid. You can imagine his reply! But, as if to emphasise his point, he said that his parents would almost certainly forbid him from getting in the car.

The phone call ended rather badly, with me hanging up as I said, 'Leon! This just cannot go on!' And I did not mean the weather...

Some time elapsed before I was called to the phone once more. The phone itself was located in the school office at Thingwall – not the environment in which to have a disagreement or even a personal conversation. Before I could speak, I heard Leon say in a very firm voice, 'June, listen, just listen! My parents would like you to come to tea at our place next Saturday and they have agreed to accept you.'

At this point, I should add a quick parenthesis ... Had Leon been writing this, he would have claimed that when I answered the phone I said, 'Leon, do you want to marry me?' He loved to tell people I'd proposed to him even though it wasn't a Leap Year. I've always denied this, but I will leave it to you, the reader, to choose which version of events you prefer to believe. Either way, I wasn't sure what to make of what he was saying. It was a shock – a great shock! And the words I'd long waited to hear rang in my ears... *They have accepted you.*

* * *

The following Saturday, I was invited to the Bernicoffs' house. That afternoon, Leon drove over to Liverpool in the car his parents had bought him to pick me up and take me to Ellesmere Port. We walked through the shop, which was on the ground floor and was still open, and Leon introduced me to the manageress, Miss Evan, who

Grumpy baby Leon, six months old on 5th May 1935.

Me aged eight with my little brother Keith on his first birthday, 5th August 1945.

Cheeky little Leon demanded a ball for this photo shoot! Two years old in 1936.

Eight-year-old schoolboy Leon with his squiffy tie! At The King's School, Chester, in 1943.

School days – me aged 13 in 1950, when I was at Tredegar Grammar School in South Wales.

All dressed up for the College Ball – diamanté necklaces were all the rage in December 1955!

21-year-old Glenda and I on a trip to Middleburg, in Holland. August 1958.

Little Moreton Hall, July 1956, our early courting days. This was my first ever shop-bought dress – my mother had made them for me up until this point.

Leon and I outside college, Spring 1956.

Young and carefree at the college Christmas Ball, December 1956. I'd borrowed the dress from my friend Lillian (far right), as I'd left mine on the train – never to be seen again! Clockwise from top left: Glenda, Leon, me, Ian, Enid, Randy, Marion, Graham, Pam, an unknown photo-bombing partygoer and Lillian.

Dapper Leon at army summer camp. Lippitts Hill, near Chingford, in 1954.

Leon and his army pals at Lippitts Hill.

Leon as football captain at The King's School, Chester, in 1952. Can you spot him? (Second row, second from right.)

At the summit of Mount Snowdon during the summer of 1956. Picture taken just after I'd nearly fallen off!

Cutting the cake! Our wedding day. Tredegar Registry Office, August 1st 1960.

Our first photo as a married couple.

Wedded bliss – two years married. Here we'd just found out I was pregnant. Gower coast, 1962.

Happy first birthday, Julie! 20th January 1966. Pictured with big sister Helen (left).

A day out with Daddy, sightseeing in Liverpool, 1968. L-r: Leon, Julie and Helen.

A proud moment! Helen's graduation from the Liverpool Philharmonic, on 6th July 1984. L-r: Leon, Helen, Julie and me.

Our silver wedding anniversary in our garden at home, in August 1985.
L-r: Leon, Helen, Julie and me.

Proud parents once again! Julie's graduation at Liverpool Cathedral in
1986. L-r: me, Julie, Helen and Leon.

Our first grandchild, Frances, born 3rd December 1996, at Ealing Hospital.

New-born Sam, baby brother to Frances. 3rd January 1999, Ealing Hospital.

New-born Faye, born 5th January 1999, at Whipps Cross Hospital.

Our family in January 1999. From top left, clockwise: Marc, Ian, Julie holding new-born Sam, Frances in the middle, and Helen holding Faye.

was absolutely lovely. 'I've been waiting for the day when Leon brings his girlfriend home,' she smiled, much to his embarrassment.

We walked into the upstairs lounge, where Leon's mother, Faye, was waiting for us. An impressive dark-haired woman, with blue eyes, Faye was always very well dressed, due to the demands of the business she ran. On this occasion, she was perfectly charming and warm, and she'd prepared tea. His dad, Maurice – who was also always immaculately dressed and well groomed – came home from the market, and we sat down to eat together. We had a lovely time, the unease of our previous meeting seemingly forgotten. After a fantastic meal topped off with a delicious chocolate cake (served specifically because Leon had told Faye I had a sweet tooth), we all helped clear the table.

'I'll wash up tonight, but it'll be your job in the future!' his dad said and we all laughed.

Then, once the dishes were out of the way, we sat down again and out of the blue came something of a bombshell.

'Leon has made it very clear how you both feel about each other,' his father said. 'But there is something we need to discuss.'

Maurice went on to explain that if Leon married outside of his faith, in an Orthodox Jewish culture, he was essentially dead to his family. Although the Bernicoffs were not Orthodox, they observed the main festivals and kept a kosher home. They had expected Leon to marry a Jewish girl in the same way that my parents would have expected me to marry a Christian boy. I was asked if I had considered converting to the Jewish faith in order for our children to be raised Jewish. I replied that I had been christened and raised a Nonconformist Christian. My mother was what was known in Wales as a 'chapel woman' and her two brothers were deacons or elders in the chapel. I had also attended chapel three times on a Sunday and much of my social life had revolved around the Church. Hence, the thought of converting was impossible. As far as children were concerned, I felt strongly that as a family we would accept both the Jewish and Christian cultures. To me, the most important thing was that I didn't want any of my children to be brought up in an environment of prejudice. That was my main aim as a parent.

In hindsight, I'm not sure what Maurice and Faye's initial thoughts were about me that evening. Up until then, they had known very little about me or my background. Now, they seemed to understand who I was and what my views were. We left shortly after that discussion, but not before Maurice had assured me that I was most welcome in their home. Faye reaffirmed as much and would become a good friend to me. As we were leaving, Maurice turned to Leon and said, 'Put a ring on that girl's finger very soon.' It really was a most surprising and unforgettable night, and one during which I had apparently given a good account of myself. I felt happy and rather delighted.

I have to say at this point that once that episode was out of the way, things calmed down considerably. As Leon had said, his parents had accepted me, and they really did. In retrospect, it is easy to understand their resistance to their son marrying 'out'. The same is true of my own parents' reaction to the initial idea that Leon and I wanted to settle down together. But from that point onwards, Maurice and Faye were nothing but completely supportive and generous towards me, and the issues that had been there evaporated almost instantly. Both of our families knew how much Leon and I cared for each other, and they knew that was all that mattered. Leon travelled down to Wales to formally ask for my hand in marriage and my family were delighted at the prospect of our getting married. Of course, things could have been simpler and Leon did tell me that if I had been Jewish, we would probably have got engaged during that first Christmas we spent together! That made me realise just how serious he had been all along, and how he had struggled with the situation himself.

Now, the questions we were suddenly being asked were rather different. They revolved around *when* we were getting married and *where* we were going to live. As far as the latter was concerned, I was pretty clear: there was simply no way we were going to live with Leon's family or mine.

'I'm not going to get married until you've got enough money to buy a house,' I told Leon. He looked a bit shocked at my bluntness. But we were both quite fortunate: he was still living at home, and I was living at the school. It meant that neither of us had rent to pay so we could save our money to buy that house. That was good. And then came the question of exactly *where* we were going to get married …

CHAPTER 6

The Beginning of Our Life Together

We got engaged on 27th June 1959, my 22nd birthday. Deliberately so, because Leon wanted to celebrate my birthday by doing something special. As a result we went to the Grosvenor Hotel in Chester for a celebratory meal. In fact, we were en route to Chester when Leon pulled over in a lay-by and 'formally' proposed by giving me an engagement ring. He had wanted to give it to me as soon as we had bought it a month or so earlier, but it needed to be adjusted properly so I had to wait.

We'd chosen the ring together, although we didn't buy it from a traditional jeweller's. Instead, we visited a friend of Leon's father who was a jewellery wholesaler and who lived in a house in Liverpool in an area of town that these days is part of Student-land. In fact, at one point our granddaughter Frances lived not too far from that house as a student, which is quite funny. I had said that I wanted a solitaire and this man had narrowed it down to a choice of three. In the end I chose the one that I am still wearing today – a diamond solitaire in a claw setting, with gold shank and platinum shoulders.

In July, just after we'd become engaged, my parents and my brother Keith visited Blackpool for the weekend. Leon and I went to see them on the Sunday and we'd suggested that this would be a good opportunity for both sets of parents to meet. We collected my parents and brother from Blackpool and drove over to Morecombe for the afternoon and Maurice and Faye joined us there for afternoon tea. There was lots of chatter and laughter, and we were amazed how well everyone got on. The afternoon passed very quickly. Soon it was time for everyone to leave and affectionate goodbyes were said. 'Our parents get on better with each other than they do with us!' joked Leon as we headed home.

After our engagement, the questions of date, place and reception still remained. Apparently, a bank holiday was the best time as Leon's parents' shop was closed and my father was on holiday, so it seemed an ideal choice. Eventually, we set the date for 1st August, which was just over a year after we got engaged. We decided a quiet civil wedding would be the most practical and it would take place in my hometown of Tredegar.

There was simply no way I could get married in the chapel I grew up in, so I had to break the news to my parents and I was pretty nervous about it.

'It'll be a funny sort of wedding then,' my mother observed.

We then told Leon's parents, who agreed it was the only option, although they would have liked a grander affair to invite their business associates to.

'Is there a kosher restaurant in Tredegar?' asked Faye.

'I'm afraid not,' I replied.

In the end we decided the reception would be hosted in my parents' house and we would do the catering ourselves. It would be a small affair because the house itself wasn't big, but that didn't bother Leon and I in the slightest. After all, it was *our* wedding day and we were quite happy to get the ceremony out of the way so we could actually start our lives together properly. At college, things had been different – it was almost as if we'd existed in this bubble – but after we left, things had been quite fraught. Once we'd set the date, though, Leon was quite open about how he felt about everything: 'June, I just want to look after you now, and settle down. That's what I've always wanted.' To be honest, that was how we both felt.

On my wedding day, I ended up getting up at five o'clock in the morning to make sure the trifles we were due to serve as part of the dessert were done, and that everything else was in order. I think there were 30 guests at the wedding and to me, that seemed like plenty of people.

Leon's uncle Harry couldn't come because his wife Bertha was ill, but other than that, everyone we wanted to be there came. I was a bit apprehensive because Leon's family were quite wealthy and they were coming to this small house, but I also realised my parents had put themselves out quite considerably over all this. They had also gone along with absolutely everything that we wanted – most specifically a civil wedding – as well as taking care of all the catering.

The night before the wedding, Leon stayed with my uncle Bill and auntie Gwenyth, and I stayed at home. My mother and father welcomed Leon's family warmly on the Sunday. They entertained them handsomely before my mother ushered everybody out in the evening on the grounds that it was unlucky for the bride and groom to be together on the night before the wedding.

The next morning, I got ready with Glenda's help. My wedding outfit was quite unpretentious in the end. Originally, I'd gone to Cardiff with Glenda, my cousin Marilyn and my mother to look for a wedding dress, but, in all honesty, I'd already decided that I wanted something that was quite practical. After we'd looked in the first few bridal shops, I knew that it was pretty unlikely I'd find anything there that was really suitable. Leon's mother found out and offered to look for something for me too, but, again, there wasn't anything that felt right. As the process of finding a dress wore on, I could tell my mother was becoming a little frantic over the whole situation, so in the end Glenda and I went to Liverpool and I bought a dress that was simple. It was white, below the knee, and with three-quarter sleeves.

Glenda was my witness and she had gone off to Paris with Ken for a weekend and bought a dress there which was white, sleeveless and with blue embroidery around the hemline. Up until that point she'd never worn it because the weather had been too cold, so she plumped for it as the dress to wear at our wedding. My cousin, who was my bridesmaid, bought one to match, and then we all bought matching hats. To be honest, we weren't quite sure about them and we all felt that they looked like meringues, but that was our wedding wardrobe sorted!

Another one of my cousins, Warneford, came to drive us to the registry office, and as we got to a set of traffic lights, he stopped. The lights changed once, then twice, and a third time.

'What *are* you doing?' I asked.

'A bride always has to be late!' he answered, 'so I am making sure that you are.'

In the end, we got to the registry office just about on time. When it came to the service itself, it turned out that Leon and Bob O'Callaghan, his best friend, were standing in the wrong place. They had to swap them around, otherwise I could just as easily have married Leon's best man! Then, as we began to take our vows, we heard the roll of thunder and an almighty crack of lightning outside. Later, of course, Leon would joke about this and he'd often say that it was a reflection of how we lived our lives together. Looking back, it might have felt quite ominous but we weren't particularly superstitious, nor did we really care. We were actually getting married, at last!

Once the ceremony was over, we had to pay the licence fee. It cost 7 shillings and 6 pence, but Leon only had a £5 note on him. Because it was the first wedding of the day, the registrar didn't have any change, so my father had to step in and pay. He actually found it quite amusing, but that didn't stop him from poking fun at Leon.

'I came here to give my daughter away,' he said. 'And I've ended up paying for you to take her away!'

Of course, we all burst out laughing, much to Leon's general embarrassment. But I felt a deep sense of happiness combined with relief and, after the photographs were taken, we headed back to my parents' house for the reception. As it turned out, everybody seemed to have a good time. Bob did his best man speech, which was very funny and only served to mildly embarrass Leon further, and then my father did his speech, where he regaled all and sundry with stories from my childhood. He also mentioned how proud he and my mother were of me and the fact that I was the first member of the Edwards family to go on to higher education and become a teacher. He recalled that I had applied myself from a young age to any challenge that was placed before me, referring to the days when I used to tackle the great stone steps en route to collect the bread at the age of three. '"I can manage," she used to say. And she has managed ever since.' It was a lovely speech, with only a few moments of mild embarrassment.

Leon and I enjoyed the rest of the reception but at about quarter to one, he turned to me and said, 'June, I think I've had enough of this now. Shall we just go?'

As we prepared to leave, Leon spoke to my parents. 'I promise to look after her,' he said.

* * *

Sunny Bournemouth was our chosen destination for the honeymoon. Leon's parents had recommended The Carlton, a hotel which his cousin Harold had raved about. As a result, we'd booked ourselves in, even though we had no idea what it was really like.

By the time we had said our goodbyes to our families it was close to two o'clock, and we drove off from Tredegar in Leon's car with the customary trail of tin cans rattling away behind us. Leon – who had been smartly dressed, as usual – was wearing formal shoes, so, while we were driving through the Forest of Dean, he decided to pull over to change them. He took his case out of the boot and opened it. All of a sudden it was if he'd been hit by an explosion! Confetti flew into his face and as the wind caught hold of it, up into the air. Clearly, Bob had been busy!

Once I'd dusted Leon down, our journey continued, and after four and a half hours' driving, we got to Bournemouth. We could see the hotel that we had booked as we approached the town. The only problem was that Leon couldn't find the road to take us to it! And so, between a quarter past six until about seven o'clock, we drove round, trying to make our way to the hotel itself as Leon became more and more frustrated.

By the time we got there, we were starving so we went down to dinner immediately. The waiter recommended the roast lamb, which we both ordered, and brought redcurrant sauce along with it. Leon screwed up his face.

'Jam? *Jam*? I don't want jam with my meat!' he bellowed across the dining room.

Mortified, I explained what the sauce actually was and told him to behave himself. The damage, however, had already been done. Clearly insulted, the waiter looked at us with disdain, and we hadn't even been at the hotel for more than an hour. 'What a start to the honeymoon this is!' I thought to myself.

Again, if Leon were writing this, he would add a few further elements to this story, explaining the whys and wherefores of this outburst. He would also undoubtedly mention that I locked him out of our bedroom during our honeymoon. And he'd be right, too!

I did lock him out of the bedroom simply because there was one afternoon when he had been spectacularly annoying. He'd been in teasing mode all afternoon and, as I was getting ready for dinner and doing my make-up, he kept on appearing behind me and pulling faces in the mirror. Then, he nudged the mascara I was applying causing it to go all over my face. I forced him out of the bedroom and firmly locked the door as a result. Of course, it was nothing serious and we did have a fantastic time in Bournemouth, strolling down to the beach and exploring the town as a whole.

During our stay, we also met an interesting couple from London, who were slightly older than us. They had a beautiful old Railton car, which, for those unfamiliar with the make, is an old forties automobile. Having befriended us, they took us around lesser-known parts of the coast, including Sandbanks – the millionaires' playground, already on the rise back in 1960. That was quite an eye-opening experience!

Another illuminating moment came during a dinner-dance at The Carlton, where, for the first and possibly the only time in my life, I saw a gigolo at work. I couldn't quite believe it, but there he was, this rakish young man, dancing with all these old ladies. It was quite something and, of course, Leon found the whole thing hilarious – for all the wrong reasons!

A more surreal episode occurred when we were out at another dance, where Joe Loss & His Orchestra were playing. All of a sudden, Leon's best man, Bob O'Callaghan, and two of their friends turned up. It turned out when they'd filled Leon's case with confetti, they'd also removed his razor, so they thought he hadn't been able to shave for three days. As a result, they'd hired a car and driven down to Bournemouth en route to a holiday of their own in Devon on the pretext of returning his toilet case. It was quite surreal to see them, and quite possibly the first time a best man has ever invited himself along on a honeymoon!

Even though we'd booked a ten-day stay in Bournemouth, after seven days, we felt that we'd seen everything there was to see, so we decided to head back to Liverpool. We had enjoyed our honeymoon, but we were keener to start our married life together properly. After all this time, it seemed surreal that we had finally tied the knot, and we were really looking forward to moving into our new house together and making a home.

CHAPTER 7

A New Home

There isn't a bloody house on this planet that's going to suit you, is there?' shouted Leon as we began to look round what must have been the sixtieth house we'd seen together. To be fair, my pattern of behaviour had become quite predictable, if not a little tiresome: we'd arrive at a house, I'd quite like it, and then World War III would break out as I began to notice things that were wrong with the place. There was one house where that didn't happen ...

It was Valentine's Day, 1960, a Saturday, and we were at Leon's parents' house when it started snowing. We needed to get back to Liverpool but then Leon's aunt Bessie rang and said that a house had just gone on the market in Allerton, about 20 minutes' drive south-east of the city centre. She had been to the butcher's earlier that week and had heard that he wanted to move, so she told him that her nephew was looking to buy a place, and they'd exchanged numbers. By the time we called the owner, though, someone had already been to see the house and they'd made an offer.

Leon was quite persistent. He spoke to the owner and asked if we could come and see the house on our way home regardless, then – if we liked it and the original sale fell through – we would be able to make an offer immediately. The owner agreed and so we visited it that evening. As soon as we walked into the hallway, I liked the house straight away. They say that is often the case with houses: you get a feeling. That was certainly true in this case. It was a 1930s semi-detached house which seemed very bright and it was also well looked after.

The butcher and his wife took us upstairs and their two children were in bed, but the little girl woke up and said: 'There's a lovely view from my window and there's lots of cats around here too.' She was chatting away and she was very sweet. We went back downstairs and I noticed there were two Valentine's Day cards on the mantelpiece in the sitting room. I turned to Leon and he was smiling. 'This is perfect,' I said and smiled back.

As it turned out, the other buyer did pull out, so we asked Leon's cousin, Alan, to act on our behalf. The negotiations got quite tense and we didn't actually exchange contracts until late July – by which time we were panicking – but thankfully, it all got sorted out. Leon spent the period just before our wedding sorting out parts of the house that needed attending to and getting it ready for us to move into when we came back from honeymoon.

In those days Allerton was already a rather well-to-do area and Leon and I were the youngest residents in our street by quite some margin. Our families had helped us with things we needed for the house. Leon's aunt Stella had bought us a dining room table, but we'd saved enough to buy the chairs ourselves. I had ordered them with green upholstery and Leon had taken delivery and stored them in the front room. When I walked in and looked at them, they were bright orange! Leon simply hadn't noticed and he began to remonstrate before calming down and accepting that we just had to send them back. As the delivery men from the shop came to collect them, I was standing outside our house. An elderly neighbour from across the road and her husband were walking past. 'See!' she announced gleefully, 'I told you they couldn't afford the house *and* the furniture!'

In fact, she wasn't that wide off the mark. Buying the house had definitely been a stretch for us, as it is for so many couples just starting out. We had scraped £500 together as the deposit but that also meant that we didn't exactly have a lot of money to spare when we moved in. During the negotiations to buy the house Leon's cousin had bargained his way through everything, including the fixtures and fittings, so we took the house on as it was. I wanted to get the bedroom painted but we really couldn't afford a can of paint, that's how broke we were! As a result, Leon was forced into becoming the Do-It-Yourself husband, which, of course, wasn't what you'd call his natural forté.

When it came to the bedroom, his best friend Bob came over to help him paint it that summer. That afternoon, all I could hear was this incredible amount of noise coming from the upstairs bedroom! I was tending to the garden at the back of the house, and when I walked back in, I heard the choice language they were using. Clearly, the neighbours had heard it, too. Despite this, I still couldn't really tell what had been going on until Leon and Bob came downstairs. What I was confronted with were two apparitions stripped to the waist, daubed in yellow paint – an absurd sight to behold.

Leon furiously began to explain what had happened. The room had been too hot, so they'd stripped down to their waists. Then, one of them had accidentally painted the other one's arm, which led to a full-on paint fight, ripe language and all. That was why they looked the way they did. This was all well and good, but these were men in their mid-twenties, not a pair of schoolboys. Bob took one look at my face and began to apologise. In fact, he subsequently spent years apologising for the entire ridiculous episode.

'I can't believe you let us loose on your new house,' he would say whenever the incident was brought up.

In all honesty, we had no choice: we had no money.

* * *

The cutbacks we made as we moved into our new home played havoc with elements of our social life. We had been quite used to going out to the theatre or the cinema, or dancing at places like The Cavern, where we had become members. In fact, we had to give up our membership, which was a shame because music was about to change and in the next 18 months or so, The Beatles would become the club's most celebrated stars.

In those days, The Cavern was alcohol-free and no one was really bothered about that. You'd go there to dance, and then you'd walk up from the centre of town up towards our end of town, which is about three miles south-east of the centre. We'd stop off for a coffee on the way at a place called The Studio.

'Would you like a Turkish coffee?' the man who ran The Studio once asked.

'Oh, yes, please!' I replied, feeling rather posh. In all honesty, I had no idea what a Turkish coffee actually was, but it just seemed exotic. I suppose when you're young, you do try and act sophisticated and only years later do you get the chance to look back and laugh at your younger self.

Even though we'd been forced to tighten our belts, we did try and go out dancing once a month, quite often to The Rialto, which was on the way into town in Toxteth – the area of Liverpool where riots took place in the eighties.

In those days it was not a prosperous neighbourhood and they had really great big bands who would play The Rialto, including Joe Loss & His Orchestra, who we'd already seen on our honeymoon. Occasionally, we would also go and see some of Leon's old friends in Chester and we'd agree to meet them for *a* drink because that was all we could afford. That didn't stop them from getting drunk as lords, though!

When it came to work, I had given up my position at Thingwall Special School because it was residential work. I had offered to go in and help out if they needed, especially on Visiting Sunday. That was always a difficult day for the staff because a lot of the kids had their parents visiting them, but there were always those whose parents didn't want to come and see them. Obviously, that was incredibly upsetting and it was our job to try and comfort those children and make sure that in some way they were OK.

Our families were incredibly supportive during those early days. My family hadn't seen the house so they came up in the September. Dad took a week off work in order to do that and his sister Maud dropped him and the rest of my family off at our place en route to her holiday in Blackpool. When they walked into the house, they were amazed at what they saw. 'It really is the best house in the world,' enthused my father, which made me feel so incredibly proud.

As well as having my parents come up from South Wales to visit, we used to go to Leon's parents in Ellesmere

Port every Friday for the traditional Shabat dinner. We ate chopped liver, chicken soup with kneidlach (dumplings) followed by roast chicken. Leon loved that! We had a lovely evening with them. On Saturdays, Leon used to go to the match and it meant that I really didn't see him all day. He'd go out early in the morning because he'd started coaching the local school team. If they were playing at home, he went to check that the nets were up and that the pitch had been properly marked out. Then, in the afternoon, he'd go and watch Everton if they were playing at home.

By that point, Leon was teaching at Dingle Vale Secondary Modern for Boys and he got a promotion around that time, becoming finance officer. The title sounded quite grand and he was in charge of assorted school funds. Just as importantly, as far as he was concerned, was the fact that he was also in charge of the tuck shop. That meant he got free biscuits at Christmas – something he was thrilled by and rather boastful about!

Leon was also very proud of our new home, so for the first few weeks, he invited everybody he knew to come round. That meant we had a steady trail of visitors every night. It also meant we were forced to entertain a seemingly endless procession of people. We were the first couple in our peer group to buy our own place, so everybody wanted to come round and see it, and Leon found it hard to refuse. In the end, I told him it had to stop because entertaining people in itself was expensive. After a month or so, he restricted himself to having his friends round on a Monday night. They would bring a couple of beers with them, and they chatted while I did the ironing.

Bob, of course, was a permanent fixture when it came to our visitors. He had also met his wife-to-be, Maria (who we just called 'Marie'). She was Irish and Bob had forewarned her about Leon.

'He is great. Leon's my best friend, but he's also really tactless and he might say something you might not expect, so please don't be surprised or shocked,' he told Marie.

All that did was put the poor girl on edge. Of course, when she did come round, Leon was charm personified, but, typically, his reputation preceded him. That, it seems, always happened!

For a while Bob and Maria lived in Liverpool, but after a year, they bought a house in Ellesmere Port. We would go and visit them every fortnight and in return, they would come and see us, so we kept in constant touch. Bob had been Leon's best man, and Leon returned the favour when Bob and Maria got married in August 1964. We celebrated anniversaries and birthdays, and we went on holiday together. Eventually, they had three children whom we effectively regarded as nephews and niece (Leon was, of course, always 'Uncle Leon' in their eyes and I was 'Auntie June'). We were very close and whenever we visited Bob and Maria, Leon would always bring the kids a packet of sweets. It was only years later that they admitted how much of a treat that was. They also mentioned that Leon would leave the adults talking and would go and talk to them as equals, never talking down to them.

Tragically, Maria died at the age of 45 from cancer, having battled the dreadful disease for four years. It was the day before their eldest son Michael's 16th birthday. Bob's other children, Caiti and Mathew, were only 14 and nine respectively. That moment changed our whole lives and Bob's in particular, of course. But Maria had made it clear that life must go on. The last thing she had said to us was, 'Please make sure the children are OK.' We were determined to do that and Leon, in particular, really tried to help Bob and be involved in the children's lives. All three have done remarkably well and we are so proud of them and of Bob, who brought them up on his own and worked tirelessly too.

Once the children had grown up, Bob retired to Prestatyn, but he and Leon kept in touch the whole time. In a lot of ways, Bob is the opposite of Leon – he loves walking, cycles at least ten miles a day and has good eating habits. In that respect he always used to despair of Leon! A few years ago, though, Bob fell ill and Leon got a phone call from Bob's daughter Caiti, saying that he'd been taken into hospital and that he was on his way to the neurology department to have an operation. She wanted Leon to know because the pair were so close. Leon went silent and became quite distraught as he spent the night waiting for news. Thankfully, Bob was fine and when we went to see him the next day, you would never have guessed he'd had an operation.

When Leon ended up in hospital in December 2017, I called Bob and he went to see him. In fact, he saw Leon the night before he died. Once he'd finished his visit, Bob rang me and we spoke.

'I just didn't know what to do, June,' he said helplessly.

In fact, he had sat with Leon and talked to him about their childhood, the places they'd been, the people they knew and the adventures and scrapes they'd had. He reminded Leon of the time they chased a horse round a nearby field for no apparent reason; of their nights out at the cinema throwing empty ice-cream cartons from the back row and pointing at other people when their unsuspecting victim looked round in anger; and of the time when they disobeyed Leon's father by taking the car into Chester on one of their nights out. Apparently, they'd parked it on a hill, only for it to roll down and destroy a bollard and the car's bumper in one fell swoop! Bob wasn't sure whether Leon had smiled at this flood of memories, but one thing was undoubtedly true: they were best friends until the very end.

CHAPTER 8

Where We Belong

*L*iverpool is a unique city. It has a personality of its own and that personality is undoubtedly shaped by the unique attitude of the people who live in the city itself. The question of just how you describe that attitude is quite a tough one. There is an openness about the place and a distinct sense of local pride too. That was really evident from the reaction we received when Leon and I first started filming *Gogglebox* in March 2013. The local people we encountered liked the fact that we behaved like Scousers, we swore like Scousers, and we also managed to portray Liverpool in a good light. Then again, why wouldn't we? It was our home for over 60 years.

I arrived in Liverpool in the summer of 1957, when Glenda and I qualified from Alsager. She and I moved in together and lived in the upstairs part of a house near Anfield. We didn't have much money once we'd paid the rent, but we pooled £1 each as our housekeeping money for the week. That covered everything, including food. In those days, there was a chain of grocers called Irwins and there was one right near us. There was a guy in there who was quite fascinated by these two young girls who kept on popping into his shop, so he kindly said he'd take care of our food order on a weekly basis. Every Friday, he would get everything ready for us and all we needed to do was pop in the shop and pick up the order itself. That was incredibly nice of him.

One particular week, however, we got to a Thursday and all we had left was a bit of bread, and we had next to nothing in the kitty. Glenda had told me she was going to be late that evening because she was taking care of a play centre session after school, so I told her I'd sort out what we could have for tea. I walked into Irwins and told our regular chap our predicament.

'I've got 1 shilling and 8 pence to spend,' I informed him.

'That's fine,' he said. 'That's enough for a tall tin of pilchards and a tall tin of golden plums. How's that?' Well, *that* was our tea! With a slice of toast thrown in from the loaf we had left. Thinking back, we were literally on the breadline!

This young chap's attitude was fairly symbolic of the times. There was this sense right across the city that, when times were tight, people looked out for each other, or tried to help. It was that sense of community that meant that Glenda and I felt at home very quickly in Liverpool, even though it was so much bigger than Tredegar.

At college I'd also got on very well with the Liverpudlians who were studying at Alsager. One of them lived further down the road from us, so we would see her occasionally and that also helped us settle in. She used to take me home at various points for a cup of tea or something to eat, and she was also the person who took me to The Playhouse Theatre for the first time. The Playhouse had once been a music hall before being converted into a theatre, and to me back then, it seemed very grand. Whenever we went to the theatre, once the play was over people would ask whether you'd enjoyed what you'd seen and they'd want to have a discussion about it. That was another trait of the city: the people of Liverpool love to talk! You could say that Leon – who was born in a nursing home in Rose Lane on Mossley Hill, just south of the city centre – was very much proof of that! So too was his ability to be quite forthright – a trait that possibly endeared him to television viewers in later life!

As well as their love of conversation and their disarming honesty, the people of Liverpool also love going out and making the most of life. Glenda and I soon noticed that when we arrived. We spent the first few months discovering different parts of the city, and, on various occasions, we'd stay out until fairly late. Of course, we felt guilty when we did because we were worried about disturbing our downstairs neighbour, who was this sweet old lady. Or at least we thought she was.

One day, following an outbreak of Asian flu across the city, Glenda had to go home early as she was so ill. I got back much later and asked if she was alright. She told me there was something far worse going on than that.

'I got home and the kitchen was really hot,' she said. 'I felt the cooker and all the rings had been on, so I've burnt my hand.'

We were both stunned because neither of us had used the cooker that morning. The oven had been used too, and we never used that because gas was still so expensive in those days. We were fairly mystified by the whole thing. It turned out that while we were out at work, the old lady downstairs used to pop up and use our kitchen.

When our gas bill finally arrived, it was massive and I wasn't sure how to pay it. Luckily, I had some money that my grandmother had given me so I used that, but we decided that we had to go and speak to the old lady about this, despite having very little evidence.

'I don't know what you're talking about,' she said, denying everything. 'I can't even get up the stairs.'

After eventually paying the exorbitant gas bill, we knew we had to move out. Help came from an unexpected source. One of my colleagues at Butler Street was leaving and told me she lived at Thingwall. The Liverpool Education Department were currently looking for a replacement for her (effectively, her second job) and she asked if I would be interested. I said I was, but that it was both Glenda and I who needed a place to live.

A week or so later, we were invited to supper at Thingwall, an old house set in its own grounds in Knotty Ash (the area to the east of Liverpool made famous by Sir Ken Dodd, who incidentally lived opposite the school). Glenda and I made our way up the drive, rang the doorbell and were shown in by my colleague, who led us to a very large staffroom, where a number of comfortable armchairs were arranged around a roaring coal fire. At the other end of the room was a very large table dressed with an immaculate white tablecloth and linen napkins, set out for supper. This was a world away from our upstairs flat in Anfield.

A grey-haired lady, dressed in tartan, came to meet us and was introduced as Miss Campbell, the matron. She spoke in a soft Scottish accent and welcomed us warmly, informing us that supper would be served at 7:30pm. She also began to outline the job itself.

Essentially, in return for being on duty for 15 hours per week, we would receive free board and lodgings – the latter consisting of a fully furnished large bedroom. This seemed too good to be true. Teachers worked in pairs and we were expected to work on Mondays (4:30pm until 10:30pm), Fridays (4pm until 10:30pm) and then on alternate weekends, when we would work from 8:30am until 10:30pm (with a two-hour break in the afternoon). We had to have our meals with the children, entertain them, supervise the play area, take them out and to church on Sunday. In the event of an emergency, we were the designated responsible adults as we were qualified teachers. All of this sounded quite straightforward to us both.

Once Matron had finished explaining the role, the rest of the staff arrived. They consisted of the resident cook, three care assistants and a duty teacher. All of them were at least 30 years our senior. Later, this would be pointed out to us – especially in relation to the care assistants to whom we were effectively senior in role. Diplomacy in dealing with colleagues who are older than you was what was clearly required.

That evening, after a delicious home-cooked two-course supper, we left Thingwall, having been told to think about whether we wanted to commit to the job. We were told to

let Miss Campbell know if we were. We thanked everyone for their hospitality and the warmth they'd shown in
welcoming us. Really, there was no discussion to be had.
We were allowed to keep our day jobs – me at Richmond
Special School and Glenda at Northumberland School –
and also work at Thingwall. A few weeks later, we moved
in. Looking back, it was an experience that we were both
incredibly grateful for and that neither of us would have
missed, despite all the hard work and the emotional inci-
dents which we witnessed there. Some of the children that
we looked after at Thingwall were as young as eight years
old and they were incredibly upset when they arrived at
the school. It took them a while to acclimatise to living in a
residential school away from their families, and it was our
job to help them. Equally, there were times when certain
parents missed visiting Sunday too, causing further upset
to the children that were waiting for them, and we had to
try and comfort those too.

Despite these situations that we found deeply upsetting
ourselves, I was grateful to my colleague too for mention-
ing the school in the first place. Then again, that was
Liverpool in those days: people genuinely did look out for
each other. In fact, they still do.

* * *

Music is also a huge part of Liverpool's cultural identity and in 1957, music was everywhere. I used to listen to Radio Luxembourg's Top 20 countdown on a Sunday night to hear what was happening in pop music, but jazz was also still very much the music of the day, so we'd go and see people like Johnny Dankworth and Humphrey Lyttelton at places like Crewe Town Hall, which wasn't very far away. In fact, I think I also saw Acker Bilk, the jazz clarinettist, at The Cavern in what was probably early 1958.

The club itself had opened a year earlier in a cellar on Mathew Street, and Lonnie Donegan – the Scottish musician who was known as the King of Skiffle – also played there all the time. Skiffle groups were very big in Liverpool in those days, playing their homemade blend of folk, blues and rock music. The Cavern also hosted sessions at dinnertime, too, which meant that certain teachers I knew would run down there in their lunch breaks, have a jive, and then run back to school for their afternoon classes. It was during one of those lunchtime sessions in 1961 that Brian Epstein is said to have first seen The Beatles. The Cavern attracted a slightly older crowd in the evening, and it closed about 10:30pm. I don't remember there ever being any trouble as it was closing. It's almost as if those were more innocent times, although certain elements of the press didn't seem to think so.

When the film *Rock Around The Clock* opened in Britain it was big news. It was the first rock'n'roll movie and the first time that a mass audience actually managed to see rather than just hear that kind of music, so it was exciting and quite revolutionary. Audiences had started dancing in the aisles, so that was portrayed as being akin to a riot when, in reality, I don't think there was really any trouble. It was just down to the fact that people got out of their seats for what was probably the first time ever in a cinema. The newspaper headlines were quite alarmist as a result!

Leon and I were still at college in Alsager when the film came out, but we decided to go and see it one Wednesday night. Strangely enough, it wasn't showing in the bigger towns like Crewe or Hanley, so we had to go to Kidsgrove, a fairly small town in Staffordshire, to see it. I walked into the lounge at college to meet Leon and I noticed he had a black eye, which he'd got from playing sports.

'They're not going to let us into the cinema with you looking like that after all the kerfuffle there's already been,' I told him. So, off Leon went to borrow a cap from a friend of his. He wore it low when we arrived at the box office and they let us in to see the film. It really was quite an experience because exactly the same thing happened that we'd read about: the audience just started dancing in the aisles, and there was this incredible sense of excitement in the cinema itself. It was a fantastic night and it felt like it was a real turning point in terms of popular culture and a real shift in the music scene.

I can't say that either Leon or I were ardent rock'n'roll fans, but everybody our age felt caught up in it somehow. Whereas jazz had been the kind of music that Leon's father was aware of and understood, this was completely new and it seemed to confirm that teenagers now had their own place in the world. It also kicked off a bunch of younger groups playing, and, of course, would lead to the creation of what they called the Mersey Sound itself.

The actual impact of rock'n'roll on Liverpool itself was huge. The Cavern wasn't the only club to open around that time. The Jacaranda – which is still going today – was probably a bit more sophisticated, because it was an all-seated venue with tables that you had to sit at. But, all of a sudden, wherever you went, there was music and new venues were opening up.

Reece's was another popular dance venue in the city centre with two dance floors. Reece's Top Floor had a dinner dance on a Saturday night, which was very popular for celebrations. I booked a table to celebrate my 21st birthday. About 20 friends came, including some of my college friends, who I hadn't seen for a year. The style of dancing had changed from ballroom to jiving, and so too had the style of bands. Instead of big bands, you had small groups. The fashion had changed too. Suddenly, you had to have a skirt that could almost stand up on its own!

Of course, the biggest thing to come out of Liverpool from that time was The Beatles, but Leon and I missed them really, because, by 1961, we'd bought our house and settled down. Leon got a job at Gateacre School the following year and he was busy concentrating on that rather than wanting to go out on the town. Equally, a lot of the staff who worked there were younger than him and, of course, they were Beatles' fans, and talked excitedly about the band.

There were lots of other Liverpool bands at that time too, but gradually The Beatles left everybody else behind because they stood apart. Then, they left the city itself. When they came back to Speke airport in 1964, I remember there was utter pandemonium, with screaming girls everywhere. As far as the boys were concerned, though, the impact was slightly different: they started growing their hair. Up until then, boys' haircuts had been simple straight back and sides, whereas now they wanted something shaggier. They also started turning up at school with drainpipe trousers. Leon, of course, didn't mind in the slightest, but his headmaster did.

'There's going to be murder over this long hair,' Leon said to me one night when he got home from school, but in all honesty, there was very little the powers-that-be could do about it. Things had changed, and that was that.

I don't think Leon really liked The Beatles at first, but as they became more popular, he grew to like them. In 1963, our first daughter, Helen, was born in April, and shortly after that, Shirley, Leon's cousin who had Down's syndrome, was visiting us.

'Can I sing Baby a song?' she asked.

'Of course you can!' I replied.

'I love you! Yeah! Yeah! Yeah!' she sang.

'That's a Beatles' song,' I observed.

'Yes. I love them,' she answered.

So we turned the radio on and within a minute we heard 'She Loves You' playing, and Shirley started to dance, pretending to jive. That was probably the first time The Beatles really came into our house, so to speak. My brother Keith was also a massive Beatles' fan, although the poor chap was playing clarinet at the time.

'You've got the wrong instrument, you should've bought a guitar!' I told him rather unhelpfully.

Because our social life had been disrupted by buying the house and the arrival of Helen, by 1964, we were listening to music a lot more at home rather than going out. Leon's father had given us an old radiogram, and as The Beatles became more popular, we bought quite a few of their 45s and played them on that. In fact, we bought most of our records from NEMS, the record shop owned by Brian Epstein, which had become another epicentre of Liverpool's music scene.

Because we weren't really going out that much, we discovered most of our music through the radio and it wasn't long before we were listening to The Rolling Stones too. The media enjoyed stoking the rivalry between them and The Beatles, but Leon and I liked both groups. You really couldn't dislike The Beatles if you were in Liverpool anyway because they were such great ambassadors for the city itself, even when they'd moved away. Songs like 'Strawberry Fields Forever' are rooted in the place.

To be honest, though, football rather than music was the thing that Leon loved the most, and the 1960s were great years for Everton Football Club.

CHAPTER 9

Leon's Loves

Leon was taken to watch Everton for the first time when he was five by his Uncle Izzy who, ironically, was a Liverpool supporter. Leon's cousins, though, were all Evertonians and he went with them in his teens, which is why he ended up supporting Everton FC. By the time we got married, he'd become quite obsessive about the club and was already a season ticket holder. To continue to pay for that ticket, he decided he'd work extra hours in the evening at a play centre at Dingle Dale so that it didn't have any impact on our own finances.

Saturday was match day and he'd go to games with his friend Norman Schuster – also Jewish, who had also married out. Parking around Goodison Park was always problematic but Norman's mother had a friend who lived near to the ground and who came in very handy. Norman used to refer to her as his aunt – which, of course, she wasn't – and he would turn up every other Saturday outside her house, park up, say a brief 'hello' to the poor woman, and then, as soon as he and Leon could, they'd disappear out the back door so no one would see them, and head to the match.

I really didn't mind Leon going to football matches because it was so important to him. Once our girls, Helen and Julie, were born in 1963 and 1965 respectively, there were moments when we had to juggle our lives, but by and large it was fine. There was one particular Saturday, however, when things went terribly wrong.

Leon had gone to watch Everton, but he and I were due to go out with Bob and Maria that evening. As a result, I'd asked my brother Keith to come and look after the girls for the night. Keith was a big rugby fan and he was watching a game on television in the front room as I was trying to get the girls bathed before Leon got home and we'd have to leave.

'I'll start giving them a bath one at a time, please can you watch Helen?' I said.

'No problem,' came the reply from the front room.

I was upstairs with Julie when, after a few minutes, I heard an almighty crash downstairs. I grabbed Julie out of the bath, wrapped her in a towel, and rushed downstairs to find there was blood, glass and orange squash all over the kitchen floor and Helen's hand was bleeding quite severely.

'Have you got a first aid kit?' I heard my brother ask, as I turned to face him horrified. Usually, the kit was in the kitchen cupboard in an old biscuit tin, but I'd actually lent it to our next-door neighbour. I raced next door to try and retrieve it, only to find that our neighbour was actually out doing a first aid course!

I got back to our house in a mild panic, still unsure of what had happened. It turned out that Helen had wanted a drink and had asked Keith for one. He'd told her to wait a minute, but she'd been rather impatient. Leon's mother used to send over a bottle of squash for the girls every week as a treat, so Helen had gone into the kitchen, climbed on to a stool and tried to grab the glass bottle. The stool had given way and she'd fallen over with the bottle in her hand, the glass shattering and leaving her with shards stuck in her palm. She was screaming and obviously in pain so we had to make a mad dash for the hospital.

Leon came home from football and rang the bell like a lunatic, as he always did. There was no reply. Then he realised that the front gate wasn't shut properly and Keith's car was missing. When he looked through the front door, all he could see were pools of blood on the kitchen floor, so he panicked, too. Meanwhile, at the hospital they had to stitch Helen's hand and they weren't sure if they needed to keep her in for the night. She was quite upset and wanted her dad, and she really wanted to go home. Julie, though, was having a whale of a time on the rocking horse that they had for children to play on, and she most definitely did not want to come home. It was total bedlam!

In all of that chaos, Leon didn't know where we were and when we got home, he was sick with worry. The following afternoon, Maurice and Faye visited us and found their precious granddaughter with a bandage that reached from the tip of her fingers to her elbow. Helen was rather proud of the eight stitches she'd had to have, but Faye was horrified and, of course, Leon was clearly the world's worst father, and football was to blame for everything!

My brother Keith, on the other hand, somehow managed to get off scot-free. 'I mean, just imagine what would've happened if Keith hadn't been here?' said Faye. Maurice nodded and would later enjoy wheeling out this story as empirical proof that Leon was easily led astray, and never where he was meant to be at any given time. Maybe it was quite a harsh comment, but down the years that did prove to be quite true when it came to his obsession with football.

* * *

'I've never brought a girl to an Everton game,' Leon said to me. I wasn't sure if that was a compliment or not. It was October 1956 and we'd been going out for about a year or so. I quite liked the idea of accompanying him to something that he was so passionate about. Everton were playing Manchester United, the reigning League champions, who were unbeaten in their last 26 games, so Leon was both excited and a little pessimistic about the game. We hitched over to Old Trafford and when we got there, Leon took a look at the team that Everton had picked and went absolutely spare. They'd selected a young goalkeeper called Alan Dunlop, who had been at the club for a while, but who was actually making his League debut.

'Who is this bloody Dunlop?' he raged, asking no one in particular. 'It should be Jimmy O'Neill in goal, everybody knows that!' He was still whingeing and whining away when the game started. In the end Everton won 5–2 and Dunlop made some outstanding saves. Leon was clearly ecstatic, although he couldn't quite bring himself to admit he'd been wrong. As for me, I enjoyed the excitement of it all. It was a decisive win and a great introduction to football and, more importantly as far as Leon was concerned, Everton Football Club.

After the match we were meant to be going to Ping Hong – which was *the* Chinese restaurant of the North-West. You had to be well dressed to get in there. That wasn't too much of a problem for Leon because he had an

Everton scarf that he could easily take off and hide. But it was a freezing-cold day and I had a pair of boots on, so I'd packed a pair of smart shoes in a vanity case that I'd had to take to the game. In those days, terraces were all-standing affairs, and while we watched the game, every time the crowd swayed, I lost sight of said case. Leon put a stop to that by simply by grabbing the case and holding onto it rather firmly. When it got to the final whistle and he threw his arms in the air to celebrate Everton's win, up went the case and down it came too, straight on to the head of this poor guy who was standing in front of us!

Looking back, I'm surprised there wasn't hell to pay over that, but Leon gave the chap a smile and somehow got away with it. We did end up having a lovely meal at Ping Hong, but I can't say that I developed a great taste for football after that, although I once shamed Leon by going to watch Liverpool play Cardiff City at Anfield.

Despite protesting vociferously at first, Leon actually came with me too and, of course, I was supporting Cardiff. I have to admit that I don't remember that much about the game. If Leon were here, he undoubtedly would have nuggets of detail to impart. The one thing I do recall, however, was that there was this guy called John Molyneux, who I think was a full-back for Liverpool, and there was this young Cardiff City forward, who was very promising.

I saw this young chap flying down the wing and Moly-neux went straight into him and clattered him. I stood up and shouted, 'Oi, Ref! Send him off!' I looked around, quite proud of the fact that I was obviously getting into the spirit of the game, only to find Leon looking incredibly embarrassed.

'Fer Chrissakes, sit down!' he hissed. That was a bit much coming from him! In contrast, I think all the men standing around us thought that my reaction was rather hilarious. That one Anfield experience was pretty much the end of my relationship with the football ground right there, much to Leon's relief, of course.

I should also say at this point though that in those days the rivalry between Everton and Liverpool wasn't too hostile. I think it's become a bit nastier since then. Maybe that's because life itself has got a bit more vicious in general, I'm not entirely sure. The rivalry didn't bother Leon too much – although he did have a few choice terms that he employed to describe Liverpool supporters that I won't repeat here! His biggest bugbear was football fans who didn't go to the game but who still felt they could openly criticise the team. He hated the so-called 'armchair supporters'. To him, they weren't real football fans, they just infuriated him. His own obsession with Everton, however, seemed to know no bounds.

When Helen went to secondary school, one of the parents there told me her husband was an Everton shareholder. I asked her how you became a shareholder and she explained. After a while, through her, I was able to actually get Leon an Everton share. That was in 1975, and, of course, that opened the door for Leon to get involved with the club in a way that extended beyond him just being a fan. It wasn't long before he was on a committee there and creating all sorts of chaos!

When Everton reached the Cup Final in 1966, one of Leon's students got him a ticket to go. The face value of the ticket was 10 shillings, but since Cup Final tickets were like gold dust, Leon had to pay £5 for it. It sounds like a cliché to say this, but in those days we could live off £5 a week as a family and still have change to spare. Despite that, I said to him, 'Take it and go, because you may never go again.' So he did, leaving the house at five on that May morning to set off for Wembley, where the Toffees were due to face Sheffield Wednesday.

I couldn't bring myself to listen to the game on the radio at all because I couldn't bear the prospect of Leon coming home if Everton had lost – it was almost better if I simply remained oblivious. Instead, that afternoon I went over to see Leon's aunt Bessie. As soon as I arrived at her place, she asked me whether Everton were winning. I told her I had no idea. It turns out they had been trailing 2–0, but had pulled it back to 2–2 before scoring the winner in the 79th minute. Oh, the relief when I finally found out!

When I got home, I put the children to bed and waited for Leon to come beaming through the door. Instead, I got a phone call at 9pm from Leon, saying he hadn't even left London. In the end, he didn't get home until about three in the morning, by which point I had long been asleep. Thankfully, he didn't wake me up in his excitement either. When he woke up the next morning, he was in something of a state and sounded like a dying duck.

'We'll have a nice family day today,' I told him.

'Ah!' he said. 'Sorry, I meant to tell you that I've got to go to St George's Plateau for the victory parade.'

So, that was it. He was off again for the rest of the day, celebrating Everton's FA Cup win with half of Liverpool. Everton hadn't won the cup in 33 years so he simply HAD TO GO! He was so excited at the prospect that I was happy for him.

Two years later, he was off to Wembley again when Everton reached the Cup Final once more. This time they played against West Bromwich Albion and they lost one–nil, so it was a more sedate affair. He and Peter went by train this time so they were spared the arduous drive back after a Wembley defeat. But such was his passion for the club that he bought season tickets for himself and the girls, and they enjoyed going to games with their dad. Helen kept hers for a very long time, although Julie was less keen. By the time he started to take the girls to Goodison Park, I was back working, so once again, we included the cost of the tickets in our household budget and made provisions for that.

As well as his staunch support of Everton, Leon's other big footballing passion was coaching the school team. In 1957, he started his teaching career at Dingle Vale – which was where Ringo Starr had gone to school, up until two years earlier – and he was committed to getting his pupils into playing sport. Dingle Vale had always had a good football team because the head of the school was Albert Virr, who had played over 100 times for Everton in the late 1920s, so Leon was in his element, and really worked hard to develop the team and those who played in it.

Alongside football, Leon was also a big cricket fan, having played it and fallen in love with the game during his time at King's School. So, as well as coaching football, he got involved with the cricket team too. Even though both sports were team games, he felt his pupils could develop a sense of self-confidence by doing well within the team itself. With the cricket team, he always insisted their kit was meticulously white in order for them to have a sense of pride, too. His attitude was that if they could perform well at this, then they could perform well in the wider context. It was about making the kids feel good about themselves. That approach to nurturing talent was something he believed in passionately.

Leon continued to pursue his interest in sport when he retired in 1989, taking up golf which he played at Allerton Golf course, which is very close to our house. Of course, he took lessons from a professional, but nevertheless he had a most unorthodox swing and stance. Despite this he achieved a reasonable standard and loved playing with our two sons-in-law, Ian and Marc, although they both despaired at the lack of etiquette he displayed on the green.

For Leon's 70th birthday we all went to The Belfry, the celebrated hotel and golfing resort in Warwickshire which has hosted the Ryder Cup on several occasions. The three of them played there and Leon was thrilled by it all. While we were there, there was a charity function and the actual Ryder Cup was on display. For a donation to charity you were allowed to have a photograph taken with the trophy. Imagine their delight! A further landmark date for Leon came on 20th October 1998: the day he hit a hole-in-one on the eighth hole at Allerton Golf Club. You can only imagine how proud of that he was! I was delighted for him, too. Unfortunately, shortly afterwards he had a very bad fall which brought the curtain down on his late flowering golfing career. That hole-in-one, however, stayed with him for his entire life.

* * *

Away from his family and sport, Leon's other great passion was History. It was a subject that he was obsessed with from a young age. He was fascinated by the First World War, and wars in general. I'm not sure whether this was somehow related to the experiences his father went through during World War II, but his interest in the subject ran deep.

When he retired at the age of 55 in 1989, we had a lovely break in the South of France, but a few months later, for his birthday, I took him to the battlefields in Northern France. Leon's knowledge was utterly amazing and the guide who showed us around told us as much. Leon wanted to go to the Somme because his uncle Harry on his mother's side had fought there in 1916, and only survived thanks to his knowledge of French.

When we got to the battlefield itself, we descended into the trenches. That summer had been really hot and they hadn't had any rain for about three weeks prior to our arrival, but the mud in the trenches was still utterly horrific. There was so much of it that as we walked through this hellish environment, I had mud that reached over the tops of my trainers and on to my socks. At one point, Leon just turned around and said, 'Can you imagine what this must've been like in winter?' The thought was utterly terrifying. In fact, we were also frightened by how far underground we actually were too – it was just so claustrophobic.

Visiting those battlefields in France had been one of Leon's lifelong ambitions and when we went to America, years later, he was very keen to visit the areas around Boston where the American War of Independence had begun, and the first shot was fired. It was around Concord, Massachusetts, which is the same area where Louisa May Alcott, the author of *Little Women*, had lived. I went off to see her house while Leon took a tour of the battlefield. He arrived back at the same time as I did and, again, the guide said, 'I don't know why this guy bothered coming on the trip, he knew more than me.' To be honest, I wasn't all that surprised by that.

I think Leon realised that history itself held the key to the present in a lot of different ways. He was also fascinated by the propaganda generated during wartime, and propaganda in general. He watched the news with that in mind and I think he may have controlled a couple of his outbursts about what we now refer to as 'fake news' while we were filming certain episodes of *Gogglebox*.

When we were in France, we went to a cemetery and we saw a grave where a 13-year-old boy who'd enlisted had been buried. The boy had lied about his age, of course, and thought he was fulfilling some kind of glorious destiny. The reality was far more brutal. Leon understood that. He had copies of those old wartime posters – the ones featuring Lord Kitchener and that slogan, 'Your Country Needs You' – but he knew what they really represented.

Alongside the First and Second World Wars, Leon was also fascinated by Napoleon Bonaparte. He was one of his real heroes. In fact, when you walk into our house, there's a small bust of Napoleon in our hallway that we bought in an antique shop in a backstreet in Cannes. Leon thought Napoleon was a charismatic leader and he admired him as a great tactician, someone who helped shape modern France and the world in general.

On one occasion, Leon and I took a school trip to France. 'I'm taking the kids to see Les Invalides,' he said, referring to the military museum and veterans home in Paris' seventh arrondissement, where Napoleon is buried. He reasoned that his pupils needed to know about France's own history and culture because it would open their minds further to their own culture. A visit to Paris wasn't just about going to see tourist attractions like the Eiffel Tower, it had to go further and deeper than that, he felt.

When we took children away on trips like that it was a joint decision between us to really make sure that they explored and learnt about things properly. Of course, such trips were not without their own perils. On that particular occasion, for instance, Leon lost two children temporarily. For a split second, we genuinely thought they'd been lost to the white slavery trade! Thankfully, though, we found them again, safe and sound. But, to us, culture was there to be absorbed: it was key to understanding the world as a whole.

CHAPTER 10

A Family Together

I'm not sure whether anybody is ever truly ready for parenthood. It's only when you actually have a child that you realise what responsibility comes with that. That said, I had spent five years looking after other people's children during my time at Thingwall Special School, so by 1962, two years after we'd got married and moved into our house, I felt that I was finally ready to become a parent myself.

When we told our respective parents that I was pregnant with Helen there was a sense of great excitement because she was the first grandchild on both sides of the family. Helen was due around Easter so I had to hand in my notice at Richmond around Christmas time. In those days married women just gave up work and, of course, there was no provision for childcare whatsoever.

I had a good Scottish doctor, Doctor Yates, who recommended Liverpool Maternity Hospital and the consultant whose care I would be under. Apparently, he'd been to university with her. 'She's not young, and she may not look like your idea of a consultant, but she really knows her job and will take good care of you,' he told us during one of our visits to his surgery. A few days later, we got a letter inviting us to parentcraft lectures. They talked us through the pregnancy, gave us diet sheets, gave us these exercises that we could do, and told our husbands it was their 'duty' to help out. But Leon didn't need telling twice because he really looked after me throughout the whole time that I was pregnant. They also warned us about two very specific situations we'd have to deal with: morning sickness and the fact that my mood might change, and I could become a bit more temperamental. 'Temperamental?' said Leon, turning to me. 'You're temperamental all the time!' He may have been right, but at least now I had an excuse.

Once we'd registered with the hospital, I got my maternity allowance and grant, and that was safely put in the bank. In those days the maternity grant of approximately £30 was paid in the mother's name and you received a further allowance of £3.50 for around 18 weeks to ease you through that initial period of parenthood. At the time I was earning more than Leon because I worked in a special school. That meant that effectively, our joint salary was cut by more than half, which was a concern, so we saved that money from the maternity allowance to use as an emergency fund in case we needed it. Then, the headmistress from Richmond Special School called me in and said, 'Someone is coming up from the Education Office to see you.' They told me that there was a new head starting, they couldn't fill my position and they asked if I could come back in for a bit longer. I had to get a letter from the doctor and thankfully, he was quite happy to allow me to carry on working, so in the end I worked until the end of January 1963. Then, I was off for three months. I was bored stiff!

The weather that year was terrible and I really didn't know what to do with myself. I found out very quickly that there's only so much cooking and cleaning you really can do, so I went out a bit, wandering about in near-arctic conditions in the snow in what was apparently one of the coldest winters on record. On one particular occasion while I was out, I got caught by the doctor, who was incredibly annoyed when he saw me. He told me to get in his car, drove me home and instructed me in no uncertain terms to stay indoors until the snow and ice had melted.

Leon could see how tedious I found it all, so he tried to keep me occupied and did everything he could to cheer me up. A few days later, it was Valentine's Day. Leon arrived home from work, gave me a card and two bars of my favourite chocolate, Cadbury's Coffee Cream and Fry's Peppermint Cream. I was so thrilled as we had very little money at that time but he had remembered the date which, as I have said, was also the day we actually saw the house we now shared for the first time. Years later, we spent Valentine's Day in Wales, London, New Zealand and Singapore, but the one I always remember is that particular day when I was expecting Helen: 14th February 1963.

Leon also busied himself getting ready for our new arrival. He decorated the little bedroom in preparation for Helen's birth, although we had no idea whether we were due to have a boy or a girl. We went into town and found this Disney wallpaper, which had Mickey Mouse, Minnie Mouse, Donald Duck and Pluto on it, and which we both liked. It was really pretty, but it was also rather pricey. In the end we decided that didn't matter, but buying it blew the budget somewhat. Once it had been delivered, Leon and his best friend Bob decorated the bedroom beautifully – this time without painting each other!

We'd been told during parentcraft lessons that we shouldn't have carpets in the nursery. Apparently, it wasn't good for the child's chest, so we pulled up the carpets in that room. I was all in favour of having bare floorboards and staining them because I'd been used to that, back home in South Wales, but Leon was mortified at the prospect. 'We can't have that! Everyone will think we can't afford floor coverings,' he spluttered. So, we got some lino. It wasn't very attractive, but at least it covered the floor and we were ready for the new arrival.

* * *

My parents had come up to Liverpool for Easter, but as the due date of Easter Monday approached, there was no real sign of Helen and so, in typical fashion, Leon went off to watch Everton while I enjoyed some mother-and-daughter time with my mum. He was too busy talking at half-time to listen to the announcer but he did hear a name beginning with the letter 'B' being called out. For a split second he panicked, but soon calmed down when he was told that the name mentioned wasn't actually 'Bernicoff'.

However, later on that Easter Monday night, I went into labour and at 6am the following morning, after a phone call Leon was told by the hospital to take me in. He spent practically all of Tuesday with me but he was told to go home at 7:30am the following day when it was deemed that the birth was imminent because fathers in the 1960s were not allowed to be present at the actual birth. On Wednesday morning, at 11:10am, Helen finally arrived. Leon was waiting anxiously at home with my parents until the awaited phone call came from the midwife to tell him that he had a baby daughter (of course, there were no scans in those days).

After letting his mother know that she was indeed a grandmother, he rushed to the hospital and was waiting by the lift for us to arrive back on the ward. Helen and I returned from the delivery room. I was tired but elated. Leon leaned over her and beamed: 'She looks like a little monkey,' he chuckled.

'Leon!' I said.

'Only joking!' he said. 'She is beautiful, just like her mother!' In fact, he was the doting father from the moment she was born. There were three visiting times every day, starting at 7.30 in the morning and Leon visited during every single one of these.

In a sub-plot to this part of our story, Helen was also oblivious to the fact that even at that young age she was playing Cupid, largely because Janet Thomas, the young woman who gave the news of her birth to my brother, Keith, would later become his wife after he asked her to help him celebrate the good news!

While I was in hospital, one evening Leon came in with a big bunch of flowers – which was very unlike him. He would buy all sorts of things and he was very generous, but he never really bought flowers. He put them on the locker next to my bed and he was talking to the baby and me. The next thing I knew, this lady was running up the ward towards us, screaming in our direction.

'That's him! That's him! That's him!' she screeched, pointing Leon out to the nurse and security man who were accompanying her. I had absolutely no idea what was going on. Judging by the look on Leon's face, neither did he.

'Oh, you're the lady I bought the flowers from,' he said as he realised who the woman was.

'Bought? *Bought?* That's just it, you didn't *buy* them, did you?' she scoffed and turned to the security man. 'He just walked off with them without paying me.'

At this Leon looked even more flummoxed. 'Of course I paid you!' he smarted.

The lady snatched the bouquet back and it was then that she noticed the £1 note that was sticking out of the bouquet itself. Somehow, between them, they'd managed to drop the note into the folds of the wrapping paper, and in his excitement, Leon had walked off without realising.

'Oh, I am sorry,' he said, and flashed her one of his smiles.

Once the drama had subsided, we went back to discussing when I could leave the hospital. In fact, my consultant came round and wanted me to stay in for an extra two days because she thought my blood count was low. In total, I was in hospital for a week.

I was also slightly worried about Helen. She didn't cry straight away when she was delivered and I thought, 'That's not right!' but of course it was. When they gave her to me before taking her off to clean her, I remember nursing her and thinking, 'Oh my goodness, I'm responsible for this child now.' It was an overwhelming sensation and absolutely nothing like the idea of teaching kids. I remember distinctly thinking, 'How am I going to make this little scrap into a real person? How am I going to instil real values in her?' These are the questions that every new parent asks themselves, but which none of us can genuinely answer – Leon and myself included.

My parents came in and saw me on the Saturday before heading back to South Wales. When my dad saw Helen, he just picked her up immediately and gave her a huge hug. In those days the nursing staff discouraged that kind of behaviour with newborn babies, but he just shrugged. 'She's my grandchild! I've had two of my own, and I'm the eldest of nine, so I think I know how to deal with babies!' he said. In contrast, Leon's father, Maurice, was petrified about holding Helen when he came in. He wouldn't touch her, which was quite strange, coming from such a man who was so forceful. He was so obviously excited but he just kept gazing at her and saying over and over again, 'She's so tiny! So very tiny!' Needless to say, the two grandmothers had no such qualms and there was a great deal of cuddling and cooing from them, both arriving with enough baby clothes for the whole ward. It was obvious that Helen was to be a very indulged baby with such doting grandparents.

When I finally got back home I found there were daffodils everywhere, which was lovely and brightened things up. 'They were cheap!' laughed Leon. 'Three bunches for half a crown [2 shillings and 6 pence]!' Oh, the romance! Then, that same day, we had the rest of Leon's family round so they could meet Helen. By the end I was quite shattered by it all, but also incredibly happy.

There was no paternity leave in those days, but thankfully it was the Easter holidays so initially Leon was able to have a week off with us. Soon enough, though, it was time for him to go back to work so I was at home on my own with Helen. He was worried about me, and he also felt he was missing out somewhat, so whenever he was home he did everything he could to help – from changing nappies to taking Helen out in the pram for some fresh air. He really did do it all, and he was wonderfully attentive.

After we got home I was still worried that Helen wasn't feeding properly and I was also having trouble winding. This was something I was concerned about at the hospital, but the doctor, consultant and nurses assured me that all was well. I had also told Doctor Yates, who called round to see me daily for ten days, as was customary back then. He too had told me that I was worrying unnecessarily. On the 11th day, however, after feeding Helen, she went rigid and I thought she was choking. I called Doctor Yates, who arrived at our house within minutes, by which time Helen was fast asleep.

The following night, the same thing happened again. Leon was there this time, so he called the doctor. Once again, he was there in minutes and this time, Helen was still distressed. He took her from me and she was sick – *very* sick, in fact, all over him. 'I think she's going to be alright now,' Doctor Yates said, 'but I want you to take her to Alder Hey Hospital to make sure.' He made the necessary arrangements and Leon and I drove the 20-minute journey in silence.

We were seen immediately and Helen, after a good feed and a thorough examination by a paediatrician, was deemed to be fine. It seemed that because of the long labour, she had swallowed an excess amount of mucous. That explained the violence with which she'd been sick before we left home. Apparently, they said, there was a 100:1 chance of a baby reacting in that way. The thing I remember most vividly about that night, though, was Leon shaking all the way to the hospital. I should add that Helen never seemed to feed properly in spite of gaining weight and being a very healthy baby.

* * *

It's hard to explain exactly how parenthood changed us. I don't think you actually notice the change within yourself when you become a parent; it just happens naturally as you make room for that extra person in your life. Of course, there were certain things that stayed the same, like Leon going to football, for instance. He also carried on with the extracurricular activities at school that involved his football coaching and the History Society. By and large, though, he was also home a lot. Sundays, in particular, were a real family day – a lot of the time with our extended family involved. During the week, I made new friends when I joined the young wives group at our local church.

Leon also started to look for ways in which he could bring in more of an income. By then, he had been teaching at Gateacre School for over a year. It was a big school, with a certain amount of social housing being built in the area, as well as a community centre. The aim was to start a youth club/disco there on a Friday night. Leon and one of his ex-pupils, Phil Cato, started running that and continued to do so until I returned to full-time work in early 1972. That meant he would come in on a Friday night, have a quick spot of tea, and then run off again to go back to work. To be honest, I think that was probably the first time he'd really had to think about making more money because up until then, with two of us working, it had always been there.

It wasn't too long before I fell pregnant again with Julie and she arrived in early January 1965. In contrast to Helen, she was born very quickly and I was only in hospital for three days. While I was in hospital, Helen stayed with Leon at his parents' house in Ellesmere Port. I didn't worry as much about things when Julie was born because I'd already been through it all before. With Helen, I'd fretted so much that I'd ended up holding a mirror in front of her face when she was sleeping to check that she was still breathing, or touching her neck to find the pulse that's meant to be there but which you can't actually find on tiny babies. By the time Julie was born, I'd realised how ridiculous all that was.

Leon brought Helen to collect Julie and I from the hospital. Helen handed me a bag and said 'for Dudie'. Inside it was the shawl my mother had knitted for Helen, and which she was now giving to her sister. Helen was then taken away and given some milk and biscuits while we got dressed and then the four of us drove home. Travelling home, I had Helen on my knee in the car and the baby was on the back seat in a carrycot. Today, that almost sounds criminal! But it wasn't back then because things were rather different, and perhaps a little less uptight.

From the minute we got home Helen was fascinated by Julie. I think she thought she was going to have a playmate immediately, but instead this tiny, almost immobile little person turned up. Helen, who was a year and nine months old and whose speech wasn't quite developed, would peer into the carrycot and say, 'Oken, eyes!' She was also always trying to help me with Julie, which was really sweet.

Leon and I were conscious of the fact that now we had two children, we had to divide our time accordingly. We agreed that I would bathe Julie before he got home from work, and then Helen would be able to choose which of us she wanted to bathe her. Julie would go to sleep early and that would mean that Helen would have us to herself at times. On the whole, that arrangement worked quite well, and Helen would bring all sorts of things into the bathroom as I gave Julie her bath. I think it made her feel involved too, although she would be quite worn out by the time Leon came home.

He continued to be very hands-on as a father and, much later, he told me that he really wished he could have been there for the girls the whole time. I think he actually felt he missed out on certain things and he hated that. Of course, fathers today get given time off to attend school-related events and the like, but that wasn't the case in the sixties. In order to be more involved, Leon gave up his Everton season ticket and went to games less regularly. Watching his girls grow up was just far more important to him than football.

When they were young, Helen and Julie loved it when Leon read them bedtime stories. *Brer Rabbit* was a firm favourite, but he often used to embellish the stories he was telling and add all sorts of drama to them. Rather than calming the girls down before bed, his stories often had the opposite effect and I'd hear endless shrieks coming from upstairs. Leon being Leon, he liked to improvise and he soon made up stories of his own.

When Julie was ten years old, she begged us to get a cat and so Tiger arrived. It would've been unfair for Helen not to have a pet too, so we got another cat named Fudge a few years later. Obviously, both girls loved their cats, but I think Leon may have loved them more. So much so that they became the subject of an entire series of stories that he made up for the girls. The stories themselves were quite often based on real events but they all had that little bit of extraordinary Leon magic. He also claimed the cats actually talked to him and, despite the fact that the girls were approaching their teenage years, they found that hilarious. He started doing the cats' voices at the table while the four of us were eating dinner. Needless to say, after a while it drove me mad! 'Stop talking like the cats!' I said. Laughing, he replied, 'Oh, so you do believe the cats can speak then?' Of course even I had to laugh then.

Many years later, in 1999, Leon actually wrote down the stories he told the girls and had them published in a book. Called *The Adventures of Tiger and Fudge*, it was published by Minerva Press, which was really a vanity publishing company. It probably took him most of the summer to get all the stories down on paper. He'd just wander off and sit quietly in the garden on the bench that is still there and write away slowly.

The book was a great reminder of Helen and Julie's childhood. I think Leon was rather proud of it and we did spend quite a lot of time telling him to write a second volume, or another book entirely, but he really wasn't interested. I think he did it for the girls and while he was quite happy that a few other people had bought copies for their kids, he didn't do it to make money.

As the girls got older, he tried to get them interested in sport. Helen was naturally good at it and she went on to play everything from netball to rounders and on to tennis. Leon would also take her with him to Barnham Drive playing fields on a Saturday morning, where he coached the school football team. Helen would run alongside him on the touchline in her wellies while he screamed himself hoarse at the team. Then, at half-time, she became known for sitting on her potty while he gave his team talk. In fact, she soon became the team's mascot and then, at the age of seven, Leon took her to her first Everton game which she absolutely loved. She had an Everton sweater and scarf that my mother had knitted for her, which seemed to add to the excitement of going to the match, and I think that is when she fell in love with football.

Julie was less accomplished at sports, but that didn't stop Leon from cheering her on. She actually made the athletics team in her third year at junior school and he was immensely proud. He also knew that Julie was slightly terrified of having to run the hurdle race, so he ran the race beside her, shouting encouragement the whole way. When it came to their schoolwork, Leon and I also encouraged the girls but he would really help them when it came to History. In fact, it became Helen's favourite subject at school and he was beside himself with pride when she decided to study it further at Liverpool University.

* * *

Helen and Julie have amazingly vivid childhood memories of Leon because he paid so much attention to what they did. He was so supportive of them and he taught them so much. During her eulogy at Leon's funeral, Julie mentioned that he put Helen on a pedestal because she was his first child, and he doted on her. That's probably true, but he loved them both so dearly.

In a lot of respects Julie is a lot more like Leon because they shared a very distinct sense of humour. In fact, Leon would often joke that Julie had been made from his left hip-bone. Julie is also something of an extrovert. There was a period when she was living in Golders Green, which is quite a Jewish enclave in north London, where she adopted a full-on Barbra Streisand look and fitted in rather well! In contrast to Julie and Leon, Helen is quieter and probably a lot more like me. She is tall, with dark curly hair and brown eyes. She doesn't like a great deal of fuss being made or attention being drawn to her, whereas Julie is absolutely fine with that.

Helen has always been quite protective of Leon and I, too. As I mentioned earlier, she was very unsure about our participating in *Gogglebox*. In fact, she would often text us when the show was on to offer a critique of what we'd said. If she'd been the producer, we probably wouldn't have made it past the first series! Helen is also a very private person and there was one moment on the programme which she really disapproved of.

As most viewers will know, David Cameron – prime minister for the first four years that *Gogglebox* was on-air – was a victim of a number of Leon's outbursts down the years. During Series Two, however, Leon crossed the line as far as our Helen was concerned. 'He's a weak, weak man!' proclaimed Leon during a particularly vitriolic outburst. 'Our Helen could do better than him! They want to let our Helen become prime minister!' Strangely enough, we didn't hear from Helen that evening. We subsequently found out that her phone was jammed with texts and calls from everyone she knew. At work the next morning, she was greeted by her team, who smiled and said, 'Morning, Prime Minister!' Afterwards, she was livid with Leon and told him in no uncertain terms not to mention her on the show ever again. Of course, that fell on deaf ears!

Helen is a very private person. She's quiet, but also fiercely determined. I think that she and Julie share that trait in a lot of respects while being very different characters in other ways. When it comes to sorting things out, they are both very capable – at work and at home. As they grew up, they would also discuss politics and the injustices that they perceived in the wider world in some detail with us and these became family conversations. Helen is very left wing in that respect, sharing Leon's views on many issues, while Julie takes a more pragmatic and practical view. She has inherited the Bernicoff business acumen and pursued a successful career in finance in New Zealand. Helen is a civil servant who works for the Land Registry.

While our two girls may have ideological differences, they are very close despite the geographical distance between them, and their families are extremely fond of each other.

Having a tight-knit family unit was always really important to Leon and I, and I think our girls feel the same way. We were both proud of the fact that they have inherited that from us and made their way in the world in their own different styles.

CHAPTER 11

Teaching Lessons & Learning Values

*E*ducation is a basic right, not a luxury. Leon and I both believed that. Teaching was really important to us both, not purely in terms of ensuring that our pupils succeeded academically, but also in the widest sense. To me, education involves so much: Drama, Music and Art are so important alongside more core subjects such as Mathematics, English and the Sciences. More recently, the importance of the Arts has genuinely been challenged, but education at its best is really designed to give you a broader understanding of the world. That is why it matters so much.

I remember having a conversation with a parent who was a very clever man. He had a terrific argument with the head teacher at a school that I was teaching at over the option system we operated. That system meant that, with pupils taking the three Sciences, there was little room for his daughter to take Geography, History, Art or Music. His daughter wanted to study Medicine, so she was being forced into the Sciences as a result. He said, 'I'm a scientist, but when I have free time, I'm not likely to open a science book for pleasure. I will turn to a novel, or a history book. When I go on holiday, I will go to an art gallery or a concert. I want that same breadth of education for my daughter.' He put it in a really simple yet eloquent manner, and it summed up the importance of a well-rounded education. Children have to experience as many different opportunities as they can to learn. This allows them to open their minds and approach life in a manner that is equally open.

I think Leon and I both felt that we operated in systems that were quite rigid in places and we had to work around those systems in order to get things done and get the children engaged in the subject. To us, education was about trying to absorb culture. That was particularly important as far as Leon was concerned because he taught in deprived areas with inner-city children and he wanted them to try and see beyond their immediate horizon.

What upset him tremendously was the low self-esteem he found in his pupils at times; he felt he couldn't get them to progress unless he could improve their self-confidence. He was looking at ways of doing that all the time. With boys, he could do it through sport and he developed an alternative curriculum that could run alongside their normal lessons. With his female pupils, it was harder because the majority of them didn't react to sport in the same way. His approach was to try and nurture their interests and really encourage them. To be honest, I'm not sure that *Gogglebox* viewers necessarily saw that side of him, but that's how he was. I think we both shared a view that we needed to make teaching feel like it was enjoyable, fun and useful too.

* * *

When Helen and Julie were young, Leon began teaching English at night school to earn more money. It was quite obvious that he wasn't enjoying it so we discussed the situation and agreed that I would be the one to conduct those night-school lessons and he would carry on with his day job. That is how I went back to teaching after we'd had the girls.

While I was doing Leon's night classes, I was approached by one of the English teachers to cover her class the following week. Her students consisted of a group of 18- to 20-year-olds, who were studying Shakespeare's *Macbeth* as part of their English Literature O-level course. 'Just one thing,' she said. 'Would you mind having your tea break with them? I think you'll enjoy it.'

She was right. When I sat down informally with the students, drinking a nice cup of tea, I got a completely different perspective. They explained that at their school, they had not been given the opportunity to study Literature, as they were told that the authors they would have to study would be of little or no interest to them. 'We weren't posh enough to do Shakespeare and that!' one of them said. 'How patronising!' I thought. These were young people eager to learn, who had been failed by some of the teaching profession, and it made me determined to try and engage as many students as I could in a range of literature.

Hence, when I started teaching at Gateacre, I decided that I would take my English set to the theatre, although I realised the idea might not be greeted with a great deal of enthusiasm.

'How would you like to go to the Everyman Theatre?' I asked.

'No, too posh,' came the answer.

I'd said to them, 'You do realise that in the old days people used to go to the theatre and stand on the floor, and if they didn't like the actors, they used to boo and shout the way people do at a football match?' This, it seemed, was enough to sell them the idea. Then we moved on to discuss the plot of whatever play they were going to see so that they would really enjoy the production when they finally saw it.

Not everything I taught was plain sailing, though. At first, I really didn't enjoy teaching poetry because I knew that it had to be analysed and that was too cold an approach for some of my pupils. It meant I had to find a new way to deal with poetry in order to fully engage them. That's when I started to look to modern-day poets like Roger McGough. He's from Liverpool, of course, so that was quite an easy door to open. I'd do one of his poems, like *The First Day at School*, and I would dramatise it and personalise it by asking the class what had frightened them when they first went to school. That made it relatable, and that really was the key, because then they would be willing to draw on their own experiences as they read the text itself.

I also got certain classics for them to read. Books like R.D. Blackmore's *Lorna Doone* – which I only picked because it was in the stockroom! For those of you unfamiliar with it, the book is set in the 17th century and the plot revolves around a romance that is also wrapped in jealousy, violence and murder. The question with that book revolved around how to make something that was so obviously set so long ago gain contemporary relevance. I needed some kind of hook. Once I'd given it some thought, I realised that if I focused on the idea of the gang warfare that runs throughout the book, I could get the class interested in the other elements of the plot. The idea worked, and it allowed us to explore more books too. I didn't care how I did it, but I simply had to get them reading because once I did, they would carry on, and that was what really mattered.

As well as trying to get my pupils reading, I also introduced them to RSA English – RSA being The Royal Society of Arts, an exam board in their own right back then. I introduced the course so that they could develop the life skills they needed – writing formal and informal letters, filling in forms and writing cheques – all of which were relevant to their needs at the time. I wanted them to understand the practical use of learning rather than view it as something that was abstract and therefore of no use.

There was one boy who was bright but who somehow ended up in my set because he used to get into all sorts of trouble. Once he got into reading, though, he would lie on a bench in the school library and almost read two books in an afternoon. Years later, I met him again and I'm not sure what had happened in the intervening period, but he was helping young offenders. I'm not saying that reading was solely responsible, but it certainly engaged him and I hope it made a difference.

* * *

My desire to make teaching interesting stemmed back to my own school days when I was incredibly lucky to have so many fantastic teachers. I'd known from a young age that

I wanted to teach, and going to teacher training college was something of a necessity for me. The course lasted two years instead of the four if you studied at university. For me, the latter wasn't an option due to the fact that I'd only taken two A-levels (English Literature and Music) instead of three so I couldn't go to university even if I'd wanted to.

I was also conscious of the fact that my mother and father had spent a lot of money on me by paying for me to go to drama groups and assorted school trips, and that my dad had worked overtime to allow me to do so. They also had my brother Keith to consider, who was seven years younger than me, so I wanted to start work as quickly as I could. Teacher training college was the swiftest route to that. I also knew that I wanted to teach in primary education. Reading had always fascinated me, so I specialised in teaching that while I was at college. Initially, we observed a class for three days to decide which age group we wanted to teach, and I realised there were children from the age of seven upwards who couldn't read and maybe would never be able to do so. This saddened me.

These days, we know about dyslexia and things like that, but back in the fifties, we didn't really understand. When I questioned the idea of children struggling to read, I found that in junior school, there were certain teachers who didn't actually know *how* to teach children how to read. The children left infant school being expected to read, but if they couldn't, then it seemed as if it was almost too late to do anything about it. To me, that attitude seemed absurd – it was the equivalent of trying to build a wall without proper foundations. As a result, I decided that I would try and teach children who had special needs, which is what I did initially at Thingwall Residential School and Richmond Special School after I'd graduated from Alsager. As I said, the work was hard but it gave me a good grounding in teaching in general, and I was able to draw on that experience when I went back to work at night school once the girls were born.

It was while I was teaching Literature at night school that I was also offered a part-time job at Gateacre School. The headmaster there was very good and he created a tailor-made timetable for me, where I taught children with special needs and those who had failed their O-level English. Leon was also teaching at the school. He'd studied Geography and History at Alsager, as well as education in general. I don't know whether he had actually intended on becoming a teacher, but once he'd come out of the army, there was a sense that his family wanted him to get a 'proper' job. He'd enjoyed school and was keen on education and so he ended up at Alsager, where, mirroring his family's work ethic, he did study very hard.

Leon went on his first week's induction course in our first year there and when he came back, he said that he wanted to teach at secondary school. Having been allowed to teach a couple of lessons during that week, he had really enjoyed it. He suddenly found something he really wanted to do. During his final teaching practice in Knutsford, Cheshire, they actually offered him a job, but he was determined to come back to Liverpool.

He got his first teaching job at Dingle Vale Secondary Modern at the same time as I was at Butler Street Junior Mixed School. While I was unhappy during that first year due to the school I was teaching in, he absolutely loved where he was teaching and stayed there for five years before moving to Gateacre. That was a much bigger school and the first comprehensive school in Liverpool. Starting there was a new challenge for Leon and obviously he approached the job with some apprehension, although he knew it was time for a change and he did receive a promotion in the process.

Unlike Dingle Dale – which was a boys' school – Gateacre was mixed, so not only would Leon be teaching girls for the first time but he would also have female colleagues. However, any misgivings were swiftly forgotten as he began teaching History (the subject he absolutely adored) and started to get involved with the school's sports teams. The school had entered what was known as 'block fixtures'. That meant that each year group fielded a team which played against the same year groups in other city schools. Usually, the teams were coached for a five-year period by the same teacher and, much to Leon's delight, he was asked to coach a team.

Thanks to Leon's enthusiasm and his competitive nature, his teams were very successful. On one occasion, they won their league and one team also reached the prestigious Echo Cup Final – a competition organised by the *Liverpool Echo*. The paper itself was responsible for supplying the trophy and they also took the finalists out for a slap-up meal at one of the hotels in the city. Sadly, Leon's team lost to De La Salle School, but they did get to have the meal, which, of course, he enjoyed.

As well as football, Leon also coached cricket teams and he was equally as successful at that. But his role at the school didn't revolve solely around sports. After a couple of years, he was promoted and became a year master with added responsibility. Soon after this promotion, he arrived home one night and said he'd been to Strawberry Field as there had been a problem with one of the boys who lived there. As anyone with a passing interest in The Beatles knows, Strawberry Field was a children's home run by the Salvation Army. As a child, John Lennon used to attend their summer garden party with his Aunt Mimi, and he often played with the children who lived there too, hence the song 'Strawberry Fields Forever'. On this occasion, though, a child from Strawberry Field had misbehaved in class.

The said boy had been sent to Leon to be disciplined and he was expected to cane him. If this sounds positively Dickensian in this day and age, remember it was an accepted punishment back in the late 1960s. Leon refused to resort to corporal punishment, sending his pupil on to his next class once he had kept him back and reprimanded him. His refusal was frowned upon by certain members of the school's hierarchy, but he stood firm. He also explained that he would visit the boy's guardian at Strawberry Field. This wasn't too well received, but he made his position clear: children in care homes did not have parents to go home to and they clearly needed support rather than any kind of violent punishment.

A few weeks later, Leon received an invitation from Strawberry Field for us to go as a family to their bonfire party. Our two girls were very excited at the prospect because the home itself resembled a huge gothic mansion. They knew where it was, but had never actually been there. Both of them loved the bonfire, the fireworks and the cakes and drinks, and on the way home, they chatted away excited about the home's dormitories, its tuck shop and the 'big house in the trees'. That marked my first visit to Strawberry Field, but it was by no means my last.

* * *

It was in the early 1970s that there was a lot of talk about extending the school-leaving age from 15 to 16 years old. In the end the programme for that became known as ROSLA – an acronym for Raising of School Leaving Age. In Liverpool, an alternative curriculum project had already been developed. It was called the Childwall Project and was led by a group of teachers, including Leon. He was responsible for implementing the scheme initially at Gateacre with a small team of teachers and later, he did the same at other schools where he taught. It involves a process where the core subjects – Maths, English and the like – were augmented with what is probably best described as a social education programme. He would teach the pupils about local history, the growth of Liverpool and the development of the cotton trade, which they would find interesting because these were real events that had happened on their doorstep.

Our school holidays were often spent driving round town, looking for places that Leon thought would interest his students. He even took them to the theatre, showing them behind the scenes and then going back in the evening so they could see a production and how the theatre came to life. He would also take them to visit the offices of the *Liverpool Echo*, our local newspaper, and show them how it worked. They loved that because they came out with a free copy of the *Echo*!

He would teach them about living history too and take them on tours of hotels to show them how they worked. I don't know whether he realised this at first, but children from Liverpool are great talkers and they are very gregarious, so if they worked in a hotel, there were jobs they could really do. As part of this programme, boys who were taking craft subjects were also persuaded to do Cookery, and some of them went to the catering college as a result, so they were getting practical help.

Quite a few of the pupils we taught stayed in touch with us, and of course, when we appeared on *Gogglebox*, a few more got back in contact with us, too. In fact, after the first series was broadcast in March 2013, we were in the Costa Coffee shop up the road from where we lived. I'd gone to the counter to get the coffees when the woman serving me stopped and said, 'That man sitting with you wouldn't be Mr Bernicoff, would it?' And I said, 'Yes, it is.' So, she said, 'Leave the coffees to me, I'll bring them over.' She came over and said, 'Hello, Mr Bernicoff. You won't remember me, but I was quite naughty at school.'

'Try me,' he said. She said, 'My name then was Maureen Merrigan.' And he said, 'Ah, yes! Boy, could you talk! What are you doing now?' 'I'm the manageress here,' she said. She told us that she hadn't continued her education, but she had made sure that her son had, and she was going to his graduation. Since then, we have met him and he too has been a Costa manager. She also told us that Leon was basically the teacher who did the most for her, and for her classmates, so that was really lovely to hear.

In June 2014, we received an invitation to attend a class reunion of one of Leon's old schools. It was organised by a group of girls – now women – he had taught there. He was thrilled to see so many of his former pupils there and to hear what they had done with their lives. We both had a very enjoyable evening filled with nostalgia and happy memories, and Leon danced the night away, as he had done at the school discos many years before.

During the evening, he was presented with a framed photo bearing the message: 'Best Headteacher Certificate, presented to Mr Leon Bernicoff at Class Reunion, June 7th, 2014'. Needless to say, Leon was overcome with emotion during that presentation, not expecting this in the slightest. He tried to explain to his former pupils that he was in fact head of wing and not headteacher, but they told him that as far as they were concerned, he was the person who had cared for them the most. He had guided and influenced them all tremendously and they wanted to show him how much they appreciated his efforts. As far as they were concerned, they said, they would always regard him as their 'headmaster'. To cap it all, at the end of the night, a man who had been a member of his old football team came over and said, 'Hello, Sir. When you're ready, I will drive you and your wife home.'

A similar episode occurred in late November 2017: Leon was taken to our local pub by one ex-pupil from Gateacre, Phil Cato, to meet a group of old boys who had been in his form in the late sixties. Leon was delighted they'd made the effort and had a great 'boys' night out'. He was pleased to see them all and to find out how well they had done since leaving school, but most of all, they told him, they had wanted to see their old form master again and find out how he was. He was most touched by that.

I think Leon missed teaching tremendously after he retired in 1989. In fact, he said as much during one particular episode of *Gogglebox* in October 2013, when we were asked to watch *Educating Yorkshire*, the television programme that tracks the lives of pupils and staff at a secondary school in Dewsbury, West Yorkshire. It really was an inspiring programme as a whole – television at its very best.

The episode we watched tracked the progress of a young Asian boy, Musharaf, who struggled with a speech impediment. The English teacher, Mr Burton, took him aside for some one-to-one tuition in order to try and help him pass his aural exam. It was inspiring to watch this determined young boy struggle to read out loud and to see his teacher really persevere with him. There was an element of it that seemed like *The King's Speech*, the 2010 film starring Colin Firth as Prince Albert, who conquers his own stutter. The episode ended with Musharaf addressing his class in a fluent manner, and I could sense Leon becoming increasingly emotional. In fact, we both were.

'That's what teaching is all about,' he told me as we watched the boy triumph in front of his classmates. 'It's a lovely profession. I'd like to go back now to teach them. I'm in tears, June.'

I looked over at him and I saw he was sobbing. It was a reminder of how sensitive he actually was and how much he genuinely loved teaching.

CHAPTER 12

Adventures

One of the things we loved to do as a family was travel. Then again, Leon and I had always enjoyed heading off to discover new places. Our first trip away together was back in 1959, when we went to Ostend, a city on the Belgian coast, to celebrate our engagement. By then Leon's parents really had accepted me into the family, and once they had, we got on well. They told us that they were travelling to Ostend and we were immediately invited, along with Leon's aunt and uncle, Stella and Hymie.

They booked us into this absolutely beautiful five-star hotel. Once again, Leon and I had single rooms, with me on the same floor as his parents; he was on the same floor as his uncle and aunt. The first evening, we went down to dinner, and we were served a five-course meal. The hors d'oeuvres came and that was followed by soup. I wasn't a big soup eater in those days, but Leon's father, Maurice, had two helpings. Then he had his fish course, his main course, and then his dessert. Leon also went right through the menu. It was at this point that I realised food was massively important to the Bernicoffs and the men were big eaters.

Maurice would have his cooked breakfast – a full English breakfast, including bacon. 'Doesn't God go on holiday?' became a saying at that point, because of course as a member of the Jewish faith, he wasn't meant to eat bacon. The question endured as something of a family gag after that too. After breakfast, his father would go out and have tea and a teacake mid-morning, then come back for a four-course lunch with double soup. Then he'd go out again and have a tea and pastry in the afternoon, and then have dinner in the evening – it was quite an impressive diet!

Eventually, Maurice had a heart attack at the age of 62 and was put on a really strict diet, but he stuck to it magnificently. Leon had more of a problem with sticking to diets. When I first met him at Alsager, he couldn't cope with the food because, as I have said before, it was so poor. As a result, he'd have to go down to the village almost every night to fill up on chips because he was so hungry. Of course, as *Gogglebox* viewers will know only too well, his endless desire to snack lasted far beyond college days, ranging as it did from crackers to cheese via infinite bars of smuggled-in chocolate.

If you asked Leon what his favourite food was, though, he would probably tell you that it was a good-quality steak. He loved his red meat. In fact, his mother's meat bill must've been astronomical when he was still living at home! By the time we moved in together in Allerton, one of his favourite dishes was a good casserole. He also enjoyed cooking a lot and he liked to make a roast chicken with chicken livers, or pasta – possibly with a nice glass of red wine.

Leon didn't drink a lot when we first met at college, but he had done while in the army. He said that there were a lot of Scotsmen in his regiment so he developed a liking for Scotch. In those days he'd often drink a pint, chased down with a shot of whisky, but you would never have known that by the time he got to Alsager. His father didn't drink at all. His mother was very much against drinking too and assumed it was always someone else's fault if Leon ever got drunk!

There was a pub right opposite his parents' house in Ellesmere Port but Leon never went in there, largely because if his father had found him, there would've been murder. So, Leon and Bob O'Callaghan, his best friend, went further afield to do their drinking. Both of them had been quite big drinkers and they'd admitted that, but when we used to go over to Bob and Maria's because neither she nor I really drank, the boys would absent themselves to go for a few pints. They'd have about three in the space of an hour or so and come back quite 'happy', so to speak!

When my parents came up from South Wales, we went out and Leon would always get drunk. I don't think it was because he'd drunk that much, it was just the fact that he wasn't used to drinking any more by that point. There was one time when my parents were here when we got back home after a pleasant evening and Leon was somewhat violently sick. Stupidly, he told his mother.

'He never drank until he got married, you know!' she said to my mother. Then she realised what she'd inferred and apologised immediately.

Both Leon and Bob liked a nice whisky – a 'snifter', as Bob used to call it. But wine-wise, we discovered Blue Nun, a German wine that was all the rage in the 1970s. I also remember Bob and Maria getting their kitchen extended. We went round to see it and Maria said, 'Look what I've got!' and she put a bottle of Mateus Rosé on the table. It was a horrible wine really, and the boys would probably have preferred a beer, but at the time we thought we were very sophisticated! I think after Blue Nun and Mateus Rosé, we moved on to Black Tower, another German wine that was hugely popular back then. To be honest, we didn't know much about wine in those days and, thankfully, we learnt a lot more as the years passed. But back then we didn't really drink very much until we actually went to Germany itself – largely because it was cheaper to buy wine than soft drinks on that first trip.

* * *

Leon came home from school one day and said, 'How do you fancy going abroad next year?' I told him I'd love to. It turned out that there was a school trip being planned from Gateacre School to Germany and if we agreed to look after the students, we could also take our children along. The trip wasn't free but we could also start paying for it in instalments across the next year, so that's what we did. This being 1969, the interest rates were such that the school would put these payments in an account and actually gain interest that they could then use on the trip. In the end, we took 42 kids (including ours) and the interest became the kitty for their sweets and drinks.

On that trip we went to Koblenz, which is on the river Rhine, before going on to Heidelberg. There, we went out with the entire group for an early-evening meal in this beautiful restaurant, only to find, as we finished eating, it was hammering down with rain. With the number of children we had with us, we really didn't fancy braving the torrential conditions. We'd noticed there was a disco next to the restaurant and since we had some 14- and 15-year-olds with us, we wondered whether we could possibly split the group in two and allow the older children to go to the disco until things calmed down. Leon went over to ask the manager if this was possible. The guy came over and said '*Shalom!*' to Leon – which of course means 'hello' in Hebrew – and Alan Rodwell, our fellow teacher, started to explain our predicament.

On hearing this, and speaking a bit more Hebrew with Leon, the manager issued us with a 'come-one-come-all' invitation and the next thing we knew, trays of schnapps were being brought out for the staff, and the pupils were given a free round of Coca-Cola! The music was flowing and they all got to have a dance too. Even Helen and Julie, who were four and six by that point, ended up on the dance floor. By nine o'clock, they were exhausted and so we took them and some of the younger schoolkids back to where we were staying. Needless to say, we were in Heidelberg for another three nights and, thanks to Leon, we had an open invitation to go back to the disco whenever we wanted.

During our visits to the club, Leon befriended the manager further and they discussed the manner in which Germany had adapted to post-war life. He told our host that he thought, in the wake of the persecution they'd suffered, all Jews had left Germany. The host replied that this was definitely not the case. Apparently, there were 30,000 Jews still living in Germany – I think we were all surprised by this.

The pupils themselves loved Germany and being there really helped them learn the language. One word, though, induced hysterics among our group: '*fahrt*'. It means 'journey' and of course, it's pronounced 'fart'. We came into contact with it every morning because we'd get stuck in this traffic jam caused by local roadworks. Just by the roadworks was an advertising sign that read '*Gutten Fahrt mit Coca-Cola*' – basically, 'Have a good journey with Coca-Cola'. The kids would see it and point it out to Leon, who, of course, played along with it and would make the most of reading this slogan out in his booming voice, with the emphasis firmly on '*fahrt*'. Throughout the whole trip, the pupils would be looking out for more signs. 'Sir, there's another one!' they would scream and Leon would duly oblige by reading it out again.

Alan, the German teacher, did most of the organising, and of course all the speaking on that trip as none of us spoke German except for Leon, who, having studied it for a year, struggled manfully with the language. One night at a dinner in the hotel's very nice restaurant, the travel rep came to give Alan the necessary documents and instructions for the next day's excursion. She appeared to use the word '*fahrt*' rather liberally and out of the corner of my eye I could see Leon trying to contain his laughter but going puce in the face in the process. Although in deep conversation with her, I could see Alan was watching Leon and, as a result, was quite distracted.

When our rep used the phrase '*romantische fahrt*' that was all too much! Not only for Leon, but for all the staff, and while we were doing our best to contain ourselves, Leon just fell apart. Of course, Alan felt obliged to explain the merriment to our rep. She just smiled thinly and said '*Ich bestehe*' – 'I understand'. We were highly amused but also deeply embarrassed at the same time. That episode was retold over and over whenever we met Alan, the last time being only a few years ago. Thinking of Leon's reaction still makes me laugh now, childish as that may seem.

* * *

Our first proper family holiday came after I'd gone back to work. We went to Benidorm in 1972. It was a lovely place and the tourist trade hadn't quite kicked in, in the way that you see it on television these days. That was the first time that the children and I flew, and they were incredibly excited. Leon and I took one of the kids each: Helen with me and Julie with him, sitting behind us. Helen was telling me she was a bit frightened as we did up our seatbelts, but

I don't think fear had entered Julie's head at that point. As we began to taxi down the runway I could hear her behind me, making all sorts of plane noises and then, as we went into the vertical climb, I just heard this little voice scream, 'Oh. My. God!' That first flying experience really was quite something. The holiday itself was wonderful too and Julie learnt to swim properly during our time there. She and Helen really loved the sea and heading out with us on the pedalos.

Leon and I enjoyed ourselves so much too, and I think it was at that point that we realised how important holidays were to us. In fact, we created a holiday fund, where we saved money throughout the year. When I was working part-time and they did my schedule, my head of department used to say, 'Here comes June, signing up for the Bernicoff Holiday Fund!' He was almost right too because we saved our money for our holidays and then we blew the whole lot every single time!

Since that trip to Benidorm we travelled to all sorts of places. Probably my favourite place was Vienna but I also loved Singapore, which was busy but really wonderful and very safe. We stopped there en route to see Julie and her husband Marc in New Zealand for her birthday in January 1993. She'd moved there with Marc as he went to Auckland University to study to become a Batchelor of the Arts where he majored in Education while she worked. Julie has made a great life for herself down there, and Leon and I loved visiting her and the family at different times, and we used it as an excuse to stop off at different places along the way and experience new things.

When we went to Canada in 2001, we simply had to go to Niagara Falls and I decided to go up in a helicopter. Leon was having none of it, but I kept on thinking of my dad's old saying – 'Remember, you may never pass this way again.' I have to say that I found it really thrilling and I loved it. 'Are we going to fly over the Falls themselves?' I asked the pilot. 'Sure,' he replied, 'if you want to get sucked in!'

During our time in Canada we really enjoyed Vancouver and Vancouver Island, and then we visited New York – a place that Leon and I were both fascinated by. Hong Kong was another place like that, although Leon enjoyed it more than I did. While I was there, though, I did develop an interest in Tai Chi, which I have continued with to this day.

The one place that I always wanted to go to, but Leon didn't feel like visiting was the Grand Canyon. 'Why do you want to go there? It's only a load of rocks!' he used to say. We didn't go to Arizona as a result, but we did end up going to Disney World in California – I suppose it's the sort of place that you feel almost obliged to visit. Leon spent the whole day looking for Mickey Mouse and he

finally found him at five o'clock in the afternoon! I think
Leon actually enjoyed the time he spent in Disney World.
The hotel we stayed in was pleasant, but the food was
awful. I was looking forward to some nice Californian
fruit for breakfast, and all they had was watermelon, but
that didn't stop some rather burly Americans from tucking
into a burger for breakfast. If I hadn't been there, I dare
say Leon would've joined them!

We had a pass for a second day at Disney World but we
really couldn't face it, so someone from the hotel suggested
that we could go shopping instead. We were on our way
to Julie and Marc's so I thought I'd get them a few little
things, but we ended up in this huge concrete shopping
centre that neither of us enjoyed in the slightest. Leon's
view was that he liked America and Americans, but this
idea that bigger means better was slightly ridiculous!

Of all the places we've been to, Leon had always
wanted to go back to the South of France, so when he
retired in 1989, I thought it would be great if we did that.
At first we looked at Nice and Cannes, and we weren't
sure, so we chose Menton, which is further up the coast
towards Italy, past Monaco. We looked at the name of
the hotels and Leon spotted one he liked: 'The Napoleon
Hotel, that's it!' he said, and that was that. He didn't even
look to see what facilities it had or whether it was any

good. As it turns out, it was a very nice hotel and typically French. Once we'd arrived and checked in, they managed to find us an employee who could speak English because Leon's French left something to be desired.

One evening during our stay, we walked up to the centre of town. There was a concert on so we couldn't get in. We went to a bar and walked back to the hotel, during what was an incredibly balmy night. By the time we got back, we were both sweltering. I got showered and into bed. 'My feet feel like they're on fire!' shouted Leon. I told him to have a shower but he couldn't bring himself to do that, so I suggested he do what all true Englishmen do: use the bidet. He disappeared into the bathroom and before I knew it, I could hear the sound of gushing water followed by the inevitable exclamation: 'June! Get in here!' I walked in to find a jet of water hitting the ceiling. The bidet tap, meanwhile, was in Leon's hand.

Leaving me to try and contain the leak with my hands, Leon ran into the room and dialled Reception: 'There's been a terrible accident!' he shouted, and mayhem seemed to break out at the other end of the phone.

In fact, when the hotel porter came rushing to our room, I think he was quite relieved to find it was only a bidet tap that had been damaged. The man in the room opposite had clearly been alerted by Leon's booming voice and the general commotion, and he invited us to come and have restorative brandy with him. By that point I was soaked and my nightgown almost see-through as a result, but our fellow guest kindly poured us both a nice drink and invited us out on to his balcony, where we were able to dry off. He came from Antwerp, he had teenage children and his wife with him, and he didn't seem remotely put out at having two bedraggled English tourists slopping around his room. '*C'est la vie!*' was pretty much all he kept on saying, but he was very kind.

Of course, we had to change rooms that night as the hotel staff tried to repair the damage that Leon had done. The next morning, we went down to breakfast and the manager came over and apologised to us. 'Monsieur, Madame, you really should be having breakfast in bed after last night's terrible experience,' he said.

To be honest, it was probably Leon who should have been apologising to him!

* * *

The year 2013 marked the 75th anniversary of the Kindertransport – the rescue effort that saw nearly 10,000 Jewish children from Nazi Germany seek asylum in Britain. I had been reading about it, there were also programmes on TV, and Leon and I discussed what had happened during the nine months prior to the outbreak of World War Two that saw the mass-scale evacuation of these children. Our conversations coincided with us running into some Polish builders, who were working in Liverpool. I mentioned that I wanted to go to Warsaw and they encouraged us to visit. When we looked into it, it transpired that you could only fly from Liverpool to Krakow, so we decided to go there. As we discussed the trip, we talked about visiting Auschwitz concentration camp. It was not something either of us felt comfortable with, yet somehow, we felt as though it was something we should see.

It took Leon about a year to decide whether he did want to visit the site of so many atrocities and I think we were both unsure how we would feel. As we began packing for the trip, I was surprised when Leon put his *siddur* (his Jewish prayer book) and his *yarmulke* (his Jewish brimless cap) in the suitcase.

When we arrived in Krakow I found out how to get to Auschwitz from the city. There were coach and car options, and when I mentioned these to Leon, he said that he didn't want to travel there with anybody else. If I'm honest, it wasn't until that point that I realised quite how emotional an experience this was likely to be for him. I booked a car to drive us the hour or so it takes to get from Krakow to Auschwitz and when we got there, it was quite different to what we'd expected. We'd seen photographs but I don't think either of us expected to see brick buildings. We went into the camp and joined a tour, and the guide spoke very good English.

At the time of our visit we had read *The Boy in the Striped Pyjamas* with our grandchildren. John Boyne's book (made into a film of the same name in 2008) tells the story of the son of the camp's commandant, who befriends an inmate who, like him, is nine years old. Tragically, they both meet their end in the camp's gas chamber. The book itself is a work of fiction, but there was a real camp commandant who lived near Auschwitz with five of his children and we noticed that the house they lived in was eerily near to the camp itself, and its impenetrable barbed-wire fence.

Once we'd walked around the perimeter of the camp, we went into the buildings and saw the horror there. There is a mountain of shoes that once belonged to the inmates who were exterminated, as well as masses of human hair from countless heads that were shaved. Both of these elements – I struggle to call them 'exhibits' – have been kept as a reminder of what happened within the walls of the camp. It was chilling and utterly horrific to see them.

Then they told us the story of a Roman Catholic priest who had tried to protect some of his Jewish inmates and had sacrificed himself in the process. The Nazis tortured him for showing that kind of empathy and, while everyone has heard such stories before, hearing them as we were standing in the camp itself made it seem all the more horrific.

When we walked out into the daylight again, Leon asked me for his *siddur* and his *yarmulke* and he starting walking towards a nearby wall. I think it reminded him of the Wailing Wall in Jerusalem, which is the site used by Jewish people for contemplation and prayer. 'You carry on,' he murmured, 'I have to do this alone.' And he went over to the wall on his own and recited the *Kaddish*, the Jewish mourning prayer – it was just something he had to do.

After 20 minutes or so Leon came back, obviously shaken, although he didn't show much emotion – he was just very, very quiet. There were some Americans who were being vociferous about the number of Nazi officers who had never been brought to justice. 'Where are they? And why aren't we looking for them now?' Leon said suddenly. Of course, those officers would have been older than us because we grew up during the war, so they were probably all dead. But he was clearly quite distraught at that point. In fact, we both were.

We had about an hour for a break before we were due to visit the other part of the camp, Auschwitz-Birkenau, and we went and sat down on the grass on our own. I asked Leon if he wanted to go and get a cup of tea, but he said he didn't want anything at all. Then he looked round at me and said, 'I'm sorry, I can't go on with the next part.' I told him that was fine. He said I should go, but I really didn't want to. I went to speak to the guide and she tried to persuade us that we should go. I just told her that my husband couldn't cope with it and she clearly understood. So, I went and found our chauffeur and we started to drive back to Krakow.

On the journey back, Leon was just completely silent. He sat right in the corner of the back seat and his body language suggested that he'd almost closed himself off from everything. We got back inside the hotel and the concierge asked us how we had found it. But Leon didn't answer at all – he went straight up to the room and said to me, 'I'd just like to be on my own for a while.' I understood why. I was going to visit a museum that afternoon and he said I should go, so I ordered him a pot of tea and I left him with it. I went out for about an hour and when I came back, Leon was still very quiet, but he was reading. 'I'd just like another hour,' he said. So, I went back to the museum, which was around the corner.

That night we went out for a drink, but he remained quiet and the next day we were due to travel back, but we had the morning to do things. We had planned to look around the university, but he just went to a park and sat there quietly with his book – I don't think he even read it, though. I think the whole experience affected him very deeply and did so for the rest of his life. All he kept saying was, 'I cannot believe any human being can do that to another human being.' And I agreed.

I think anyone who visits the camp feels that way – I don't think I can truly describe the horror of the place here. If you are Jewish, the resonance is even more significant, of course. For Leon, while he had had struggles with his faith in his youth, he became increasingly proud of his Jewish roots as he grew older. When he began teaching in Liverpool in 1957, he joined Harold House, a Jewish youth club and community centre. There, he played football every Sunday during the winter and then cricket in the summer. Certainly, until a few years ago he held the record for being the club's highest-scoring batsman: 60 not out! Needless to say, he was very proud of that. More significantly, his association with Harold House meant that for the first time in his life, Leon had Jewish friends with whom he could identify and he began to embrace with pride his Jewish culture.

I realised how important Leon's faith had become to him when we got engaged and, as a result, I felt that it was important our children were aware of their heritage.

I wanted them to go to their paternal grandparents to appreciate the importance of *Pesach* – or Passover – and why they ate *matzos* – unleavened bread (a symbol of the Israelites' liberation, their sudden flight from Egypt meaning that the bread they were baking had no time to rise). Later in the year, Leon observed two important festivals. He accompanied his parents to synagogue (or *Schule*) for New Year (or *Rash Hashanah*) and ten days later, The Day of Atonement (or *Yom Kippur*). The Day of Atonement is a most holy day, when Jewish adults fast from sundown on the eve of *Yom Kippur* until sundown of the following day. Our whole family and some of the extended family would gather at our house to break the fast, enabling us to celebrate these cultural festivals together.

Our trip to Auschwitz underlined exactly why this was so important.

CHAPTER 13

Our Growing Family

'Congratulations, June! You're a grandmother. It's a baby girl and she's called Frances! Can you come over and see her tomorrow afternoon?' asked Ian, Helen's husband excitedly, as he rang to tell us the news on that December evening in 1996. We'd seen how happy our own parents had been when they found out that they were going to be grandparents, but I'm not sure we were prepared for the emotions we felt when Frances herself arrived. It was a mixture of pride and sheer excitement.

The next afternoon, we went to Ealing Hospital to meet Frances for the first time, along with Ian's parents, Maureen and Eddie. Helen and Ian had met in London in 1986 when Helen had joined the Rotaract club (the youth branch of the Rotary Club) because she wanted to begin doing some charity work and to make new friends. They got on fantastically well and ended up getting married in 1991. Ian is one of the most punctual people on the planet but on this occasion he was late picking us up to take us to the hospital because he was busy getting flowers and chocolates for the nursing staff. When we went in, we saw Helen immediately – she looked really well, and so did Frances.

The following day, Leon came home and I stayed down in west London for a couple of weeks to help Helen out. I spent the weekends over at Julie and her husband Marc's house in Highams Park, near Waltham Forest, so that Helen, Ian and Frances would be able to spend time together. Of course, that Christmas involved a big family gathering at Julie's, which we all enjoyed. Leon really was in his element and thrilled that he had another little girl to fuss over. It was a wonderful time for us all.

Between September and December of the following year, I spent alternate weeks in London as Helen returned to work. There were no nursery places available for Frances so Ian's mother Maureen and I shared the childcare, which probably explains the close bond that has always existed between us. I soon became familiar with the various parks and children's playgrounds around Perivale and Ealing. I particularly loved the walk along the canal bank, with its houseboats and accompanying wild life, and Frances enjoyed waving to people on the passing boats. Somehow, she always managed to spot a heron, much to

My 70th birthday celebrations. Paihia, Bay of Islands, New Zealand, 2007. L-r: Sam, Julie, Marc, Faye (arms round me), Frances, Leon and Ian.

Leon's ambition realised – taking his grandson Sam to the FA Cup semi-final in 2009! Everton vs Man United… and Everton won! L-r: Sam, Leon and Helen.

With our three beloved grandchildren in the front garden, just before we treated them to dinner out, in August 2002. L-r: Leon, Frances, me, Faye and Sam.

The 'fahrty' school trip to Germany in 1969. Leon has his arms crossed in his teacher pose, whilst I am third from right with my arms behind my back. Julie is fourth from the left and Helen is sixth from the left on the front row!

Leon and his cricket team at Dingle Vale boys' school, 1959.

A very proud day – Leon accepting his certificate of Meritorious Service from the Lord Mayor, at Liverpool City Council, on 23rd February 1990.

My 70th birthday –
a quick Kir Royale
before a surprise party
arranged by Leon at
the Marriott, 2007.

Leon's 64th birthday
in Paris – nobody
understood a word
of his French!

Wine tasting in Budapest, boating on the Amalfi coast, and very happy in our hats on a coffee break in Sorrento!

Celebrating our golden wedding anniversary on a family holiday in Tuscany, 2010. L-r: Leon, Faye, Frances, Sam, Helen, Ian, me, Marc, Julie.

Leon and one of his greatest loves: food! And you can bet he finished the lot! Dinner at a Tuscan vineyard in 2010.

Gogglebox bags a
BAFTA! May 2014.

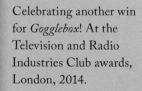

Celebrating another win
for *Gogglebox*! At the
Television and Radio
Industries Club awards,
London, 2014.

Our silver wedding anniversary waltz, 1st August 1983.

my surprise. During our stroll, we also usually called in on her other grandparents for a cup of tea and a chat.

When Frances finally got her nursery place, Leon and I got on with our lives for a while and then in the spring of 1998 Julie rang us to tell that she had some news: she was pregnant. Then, almost immediately, Helen rang to say she was also expecting. Once again, Leon and I were incredibly excited. I think that when you become a grandparent you really do look for any excuse to spend time with your children again. Your bond becomes even stronger, maybe because the experience reminds you of what it means to be a parent all over again. Of course, you also want to spend as much time with your grandchildren as you can, although you end up being far more lenient with them than you were with your own children. Leon, in particular, would let them do almost anything, and get up to all sorts of mischief with them. There is one specific incident in December 1998 that springs to mind …

We had gone down to visit the girls and we went to Brent Cross Shopping Centre in north-west London to do some Christmas shopping. Helen and Julie were heavily pregnant and also needed a few last-minute things for their trips to hospital. Rather than drag Frances, who was about one and a half then, round every shop with us, we left her with Leon by this enormous Father Christmas inflatable, snow cascading all around him – 'She'll drop off to sleep in about ten minutes,' said Helen as we strolled off.

When we came back about half an hour later, we could tell that Frances wasn't asleep because we could see her head nodding from the back. Helen walked round to the front of the pram to tell her she was back and her facial expression changed from a smile to one of horror. 'What have you given her?' she shrieked at Leon. It turned out he had bought Frances a chocolate egg filled with cream. He'd given it to her, wrapper and all, because he was so clumsy that he couldn't unwrap it. She had this egg and cream all over her face – it was in her hair, it was in the fur on her coat! Everywhere! And Frances' jaw was almost locked with this horrendous cream too and she didn't look very happy about it at all. Obviously, Helen was furious as she tried to clean up the mess but Leon saw absolutely nothing wrong with what had happened.

There were meant to be five days between Helen and Julie's due dates but it ended up being just two. Helen and Ian's second child, Sam, was the first to arrive in that January of 1999, and 48 hours later, we got a call from Marc. 'Faye Bernicoff has arrived!' he proclaimed with great excitement. For Leon, in particular, this was a proud moment. Marc had taken Julie's name, and they had named their little girl after Marc's beloved mother who shared a name with Leon's mother, and who sadly passed away before she could meet Julie or her beautiful granddaughter.

Marc picked us up from Walthamstow station and took us to Whipps Cross Hospital to meet Faye for the first time. I remember sitting on a rather shabby couch and this nurse walked over. I'm not sure why I said it, but I smiled at her and said, 'I'm Baby Bernicoff's grandmother.' She looked utterly dismissive and snapped, 'Visiting time is in ten minutes!' Julie wanted to come out of the ward to see us so Marc went to fetch her. When we saw her, she was white-faced and had this tiny baby with masses of black hair in her arms. Faye became quite poorly when she was just three weeks old with a virus. I stayed in London as Marc had to return to work (he was working as a member of IT support at the accountancy firm Arthur Andersen). Unfortunately, I developed a chest infection so Leon came down and stayed with Julie at the hospital during the day until Marc arrived. It was a very anxious time for them all.

In a short while, Faye was a bouncing baby, and she is a Bernicoff by name and a Bernicoff by nature. She's just like Leon in that she'll talk to anyone about anything. Faye is at Massey University in Auckland, New Zealand now where she is studying to become a Bachelor of the Arts in Retail and Business Management, and she works part-time in a dress shop, just as Leon's mother did. She's also very good at sport. She really is like Leon in the sense that she's also more of a team player. She's great at tennis but also good at netball. Leon was very supportive of all her sporting endeavours in the same way that he was with our girls. He got very excited when he watched her playing tennis and always used to say to her, 'You can beat this one!'

When Julie, Marc and Faye emigrated to New Zealand in November 2002 we were obviously very sad, but our granddaughter stayed with us for a few days while her parents packed up the house. Since then, we spent blocks of time with Faye because it's such a long way to go to New Zealand. We planned our visits in order to be there during certain key moments. When Faye started infant school and then middle school, we were there. We did the same thing with senior school. The only thing we missed was her starting university, and if Leon hadn't been ill, we would have travelled down for that too.

Having part of the family down in New Zealand meant that we tried to spend certain holidays with everybody. Julie, Marc and Faye have come back so we could spend the Christmas period together and we tried to make sure that Faye has been able to see different parts of England too. We once hired a place down in Somerset in order for her to explore Bath and Wells. And, of course, she has spent time at Helen and Ian's in Warwickshire with her cousins, Frances and Sam, and went with them to Stratford and to the Royal Shakespeare Theatre.

In 2009, for our golden wedding anniversary, we all went to Tuscany. We searched around to find a company who would plan the trip and ended up hiring a villa that had its own Italian cook. And, of course, in true Italian fashion, she had the kids come into the kitchen so they could taste the food as she was making it. She was making *gnocchi*, which the kids were familiar with, but when she started frying courgette flowers, they thought they were amazing and they loved it! At one point she was talking to Sam through an interpreter and he told her that he loved chips, so she made him more chips than he could ever eat. The children couldn't get over all the courses she made, but of course Leon told them to tuck in!

On that trip we took the family into Florence to explore the city, and we went off the beaten track to find proper Italian restaurants. We also visited a street festival, which they loved. There were performers on high wires with no safety nets, mime artists too, which they were fascinated by. It was a real adventure for them, and for us too.

* * *

With Faye being so far away, we were really grateful that Frances and Sam were closer to us. When Sam was nine months old, Helen and Ian moved up to Warwickshire. Ian is a Londoner and he worked in central London for Stanley Gibbons, the stamp dealers. When he got this job in Warwick, they decided to move. They were delighted because they're both great walkers and there's a lot to explore around there. For us it was nice because it only took us two hours to get down to see them rather than the four-hour journey to London. When they moved, Frances stayed with us for a few days and we took her to Chester Zoo for the first time.

I suppose like all grandparents, we enjoyed spoiling our grandchildren, and Frances used to love coming up to spend time with us. As a result, her younger sibling Sam couldn't wait to come up and spend some time with us on his own. It wasn't long before they both came to see us for a summer holiday, and Chester Zoo became a firm favourite every summer. It's a fantastic zoo and, more recently, the place where they film *The Secret Life of the Zoo*, the Channel 4 programme. They breed a number of protected species there, and the kids used to particularly love seeing the baby elephants. We would go there for the whole day, arriving when it opened for 10 o'clock so we could really make the most of it. We'd have a picnic lunch and then go out to a restaurant in the evening.

On one particular occasion it was raining so we tried to put it off, but in the end decided not to. We got halfway to the zoo and Leon said, 'Oh, no, I've got my slippers on!' Sam laughed and said, 'Your Homer Simpson slippers?' We'd left the house in such a disorganised state that Leon had simply walked out of the door wearing those slippers. So, we traipsed round the zoo with Leon wearing them the whole time and, of course, loads of other children spent time just pointing at his feet! It's another one of those stories that has passed into Bernicoff folklore and also quite typical of Leon's absent-mindedness!

During another of our visits to Chester Zoo, Sam and Frances developed an interest in meerkats – Sam, in particular, had read up on them. When we came to the meerkat enclosure, we could see one of them standing bolt upright. Sam said to Leon, 'He's on the lookout, Dada,' and then started to explain the behavioural patterns of meerkats to us. When he'd finished, this voice said, 'What's your name, young man?' Sam replied and the man, who was actually one of the meerkat keepers, said, 'Well, thank you, Sam. You've told all the children what I was about to tell them!' Sam was hugely embarrassed as a class of schoolchildren had assembled around the enclosure.

Our summers with Frances and Sam were always great fun. We used to go down to New Brighton – about 35 minutes away – down Harrison Drive and head for the beach. Leon always bought a newspaper – most often the *Liverpool Football Echo* (also known as *The Pink*) – on the way and all he would ask was that, during the course of the day, he could have a little bit of time to read it. He would also read it from the back to the front, something I think is very much a 'man thing'.

The kids loved running off and playing on the beach. Sam was busy building sandcastles and Frances was dancing around in the sand. On one occasion, she came running back to me and said, 'There's big, pink pebbles on the beach.' 'That can't be right,' I thought. And it wasn't – there were enormous jellyfish everywhere. I decided it was time to leave and we went off to play crazy golf instead. That night, there was a warning on the TV news about the jellyfish. They'd had to deploy ambulances because children had been really badly stung throughout the day. Leon and I were quite relieved, but it was all part of the adventures of grandparenthood!

There was another fantastic memory when Helen and Ian took us all to Blackpool to see the illuminations on Leon's 75th birthday. One of Leon's many claims to fame was that in his younger days he had danced in the ballroom where they film the BBC's *Strictly Come Dancing* now. By then, Frances had become interested in *Strictly*, and they were getting ready to start filming when we arrived. Unfortunately, I was in a wheelchair because I'd sprained my ankle, but Leon persuaded Frances to dance with him. She did and, again, we all had a fantastic time!

* * *

After deliberating between studying at Cardiff or Liverpool University, Frances decided to study English Literature at the latter, which meant we got to spend more time with her. The strange thing was that her first year in hall, she lived in Grove Street, which is where Leon's grandparents first lived when they moved to Liverpool, so there was a bit of family history there too. In those days it was the big Jewish quarter. Leon had played football around there too when he was younger. His mother actually lived in Crown Street – also in the area – and attended the synagogue in Grove Street, so that was a nice bit of familial Jewish history. The only cloud on the horizon was that Leon promised that he would attend Frances' graduation in the summer of 2018 and of course he wasn't able to do so.

The graduation ceremony takes place in the Liverpool Philharmonic Hall in the centre of the city, which is also where Helen graduated. 'I'll be cheering you on, Frances, in the Philharmonic Hall, just like I did your mother!' Leon told her. Frances used to tell him she couldn't get him a ticket because she could only get two, which she intended to give to her parents, of course. I told him that the best he could do was to watch the ceremony in Abercromby Square where it was being screened and where Julie had actually had her wedding reception. But he would have none of it. 'I'll be there!' he repeatedly told Frances. Of course, she would have loved to have had her grandfather there, but it was not to be. I have to say, though, that having Frances nearby and staying with me for a while following Leon's passing has been a great comfort to me.

Frances is a bit like her mother in that she has always done the things she wanted to. A 21st-century young woman who likes to be independent, she was very close us both, but certainly to Leon. She used to love cooking him a meal and then, once he'd eaten it, telling him it was vegetarian! Of course, he loved his meat, but he took it in good spirits.

Frances enjoys drama and the theatre and has done so from an early age. When she came to Liverpool, we'd go to the theatre with her, be it to see a children's production like *Charlotte's Web* or a pantomime, something all three grandchildren enjoyed. Back home in Warwick, she joined a drama group called Playbox, where she took part in some of the plays they produced. Of course, as grandparents we would go down to see all the productions, and true to form, Leon would always ask the same question:

'Frances, why aren't you playing the lead?' he would say on almost every occasion. 'Maybe it's because I didn't actually audition for that part, Dada,' came the somewhat exasperated reply. Frances always gave as good as she got when it came to her conversations with Leon and he loved every minute of it. He adored her spirit, her sense of fun and her ability to be outspoken on occasion: 'She was my first grandchild!' he used to say with great joy.

Since she came to study at Liverpool University, she accompanied us to a variety of theatre productions. Quite fittingly, the last one we all went to see was *Fiddler on the Roof* – the musical classic based on the life of a Jewish family in Russia before the pogroms. Leon enjoyed it tremendously, and sang along rather heartily to the show's most famous tune, 'If I Were a Rich Man'.

Another memorable evening came in December 2017, when Frances turned 21. We all went out for a celebration meal to the newly opened Gino's Italian restaurant. Once again, Leon was on top form and spent a great deal of the evening beaming with pride and loving every minute of the celebration itself. 'What a great night!' he exclaimed when we got home.

Alongside Frances' theatrical exploits, Leon was always interested in the books she was reading. 'This year I'm doing women's literature,' she said on one occasion. 'Who exactly?' asked Leon. 'They're modern authors, Dada,' she replied, listing the relevant writers. 'Never heard of them!' he laughed. When she started reading Charles Dickens that was fine by him. But they would both sit and talk about her work and he loved doing that. At Leon's funeral, Frances read Shakespeare's Sonnet 18, but she didn't share any memories of the multitude of conversations she had enjoyed with her grandfather down the years – 'Those were private moments,' she told me.

Leon also spent a great deal of time with Sam. As was the case with all his grandchildren, he was always there to offer encouragement but the pair of them really enjoyed discussing sport. Sam has played sport since he was tiny. He played for the Wardens' Colts team in Kenilworth. His dad trained as a coach, too, and Leon used to go down to watch Sam play all the time. The team loved Leon, of course. He was as vociferous as ever – I think he bought a pair of tracksuit bottoms especially for those visits! He got to know all the parents too and, I have to say, he was one of those awful grandparents who, if the referee made what he perceived as a bad decision, would let it be known that he disagreed at the top of his voice.

Leon really enjoyed watching children as they got into sport – I think he loved the naive enthusiasm that exists before kids become aware that a sport like football requires tactics. There is a joy that comes from watching them play football when they are so excited that virtually all of them run down towards the opposing goal en masse. They have no idea of the position they're meant to play in, but they have this joy that comes with the idea of playing. I think Leon, when he was coaching, also loved watching a team emerge from all of that chaos.

Like Leon, Sam also loves cricket and, again, he did so from an early age. When Sam was about nine or ten we dropped him and Leon off at Edgbaston so they could go and see Warwickshire play. Leon was in his early seventies and he'd just started walking with a stick. Since Sam was so young, we didn't think he'd last the whole day at the match, but to his credit, he managed it. Rather than pick them up, Leon called to say that they were going to get the train back and we could pick them up from the local station. I met them there in the car and I said to Leon, 'I hope you looked after Sam properly?' Then I heard this little voice from the back of the car: 'No, he didn't! He left his stick at the bar and I had to go back and fetch it!' I couldn't quite believe it, but, typically, Leon just glossed over it – 'I was a bit tired and I didn't think Sam would mind in the slightest,' he smiled.

After we'd appeared on *Gogglebox*, Leon was invited to Old Trafford to watch a cricket match. He asked if he could take his grandson and they were kind enough to send him three tickets. Sam was utterly thrilled. We were having some refreshments and somebody stopped to talk to Leon about something relating to the match. Once the conversation was over, we realised we'd lost Sam completely. Of course, he was a young man by then, so we weren't all that worried, but we found him back at the seats. Basically, he couldn't bear to miss a minute of the match! Leon was like that, too.

When Leon went to cricket, he didn't like it when people in the crowd shouted or acted in a vulgar manner. 'You can shout all you want at football matches, but you behave properly at cricket matches!' he used to say. He didn't like seeing teams playing in these newfangled, multi-coloured kits either. 'They look like they're playing in their pyjamas!' he smarted. I think his reaction was down to the pride he took in making sure his own cricket whites were meticulous when he played. It was also something he tried to instil in the teams he coached. In fact, when it came to cricket, he was a bit of a puritan.

When it came to football, Leon's great ambition was to take Sam and Helen to see Everton play in a Cup Final at Wembley. In fact, Sam is a QPR supporter and Leon respected that. In 2009, Everton reached the semi-final of the FA Cup, where they faced Manchester United.

Leon got tickets for all three of them and they went in full Everton colours. The game was 0–0 after extra time, but Everton won 4–2 on penalties, which engendered all sorts of euphoria. Unfortunately, Everton lost in the final to Chelsea, but Leon was just glad that all three of them had been to Wembley to watch his beloved Blues.

Leon loved the fact that he had a grandson who was like a walking encyclopaedia when it comes to sports. I think Sam accepted that he wasn't going to become a professional footballer so he said to Leon, 'If I can't play, then maybe I'll become a commentator.' One of Bob's sons, Mathew, works on Trans World Sport, the weekly television programme, and he invited Sam to pop into the office to have a look around – he loved that. Sam's currently studying Consumer Behaviour And Marketing at Reading University, so I suppose he is still working out what he wants to do.

I think both Sam and Frances were astonished when we began appearing on *Gogglebox*. When Frances moved to Liverpool and lived in halls, she watched the show with her housemates and it appears that they noticed she was rather quiet while it was on. They questioned her as to why and, eventually, she had to admit that we were her grandparents. Her friends were fans of the programme and some months later, she actually brought them round to visit us, which was great fun.

Unlike Frances, Sam was quite open about the fact that we were on the show. There was a moment during that first programme when Leon was caught on-camera in a rather flatulent mood. The rest of the family were somewhat mortified by that. 'Couldn't they have cut that out?' said Helen. But Sam found it hilarious. 'My granddad's a legend! He farted on national TV!' is what he tweeted. Of course, Leon thought that was hilarious, too.

In fact, Leon loved the fact that we were often stopped in the street by younger people, who wanted to chat. They would say the same thing: 'You're just like my granddad.' They also tended to agree with various things he'd said on the show, something he was very happy about. It meant that he wasn't the typically grumpy old man on TV. Leon thought a lot of younger people, and he believed they were often unfairly maligned, especially recently. As a result, he always wanted to hear what they had to say, even if they were people he'd just met. I think one of his favourite moments was when someone said to him, 'You're like everybody's granddad, really.' He gave them one of those big grins!

CHAPTER 14

'What if we can't think of anything to say?'

Gogglebox, Series 1

'What if we can't think of anything to say?' It was the question that bothered me most on the day we started filming the very first episode of *Gogglebox* in March 2013. Needless to say, it was not a thought that appeared to have crossed Leon's mind in the slightest. Leon had been on *North West Tonight*, our local BBC TV news programme, twice before when he was interviewed on that show. In comparison to me, that made him an old hand when it came to appearing on television. Of course, were Leon here now, he would be the first to admit that he also quite enjoyed the sound of his own voice!

The week before we were due to film we had spoken to Tania Alexander, the show's executive producer and the woman who had envisaged exactly how *Gogglebox* would work from the perspective of both the cast as well as the viewers. She calmly outlined the whole filming process and told us that she simply wanted us to be ourselves. Speaking to her had helped clarify a lot of things and also made me feel much calmer about the idea of appearing on the programme. That said, I also knew that, despite my years of teaching, I had never been the most confident of public speakers. So, there it was again. *That* question: 'What if we can't think of anything to say?'

On top of that, I was also worried about having a camera crew in my house. What would the house actually look like on television? And what would *we* look like on TV? When the first cameraman arrived, though, he was very kind. He walked in at about two thirty in the afternoon and complimented me on the lovely clean carpet in the hallway. As he began placing cables, we talked about his family and then ours, and it made me feel that even though we were going to appear on television, we were dealing with normal people.

Once everything was set up, another moment of anxiety crept in: what were we actually going to watch? And what if we hated what we saw? Even worse, what if we sounded utterly ridiculous discussing what we'd watched? I was very aware that I might say things that sounded plain silly. Leon told me not to be so ridiculous, he just seemed to be taking it all in his stride. Then, I started worrying about what Leon might have to say about the programmes we were watching!

Eventually, when we finally began filming later that day, it did all feel surprisingly normal. Tania had told us that there would be a break during the filming and that would be a good time for us to eat our evening meal. We'd been and got a ready meal from Marks & Spencer in preparation and we'd all had a nice cup of tea before the cameras started rolling. That had settled us and everybody else down rather nicely. The room people see on TV is the one we used from that very first day onwards, and as I subsequently found out, it really doesn't look any different on television. The only thing we had to change was the position of the couch. Normally, that would've been next to the table to the right of Leon's chair, but it had to be replaced by a chair for me to sit in. Other than that, it really did feel as if we were sitting in our lounge watching television, and bar the odd whirr of the camera, after that first show it really didn't feel too strange at all.

Sometimes we'd come back in after taking a break from filming and we'd be sat slightly differently and so the production team would re-set the shot and make sure we were in the right position. As we got used to filming during that first series, there was the odd moment of mischief from Leon – like the time he tried to sneak his mug with a massive Everton crest on it into the shot – but otherwise it was all very natural and felt as though we were just watching TV.

The first episode of *Gogglebox* was broadcast on Thursday, 7th March 2013, at 10pm. Leon was very excited about watching it, and I was too, although I was still incredibly nervous and asking myself an almost infinite amount of questions. We had told Helen, Julie and my brother Keith and his daughter Claire about the show being on, but that was about it. I wasn't too bothered about people we didn't know watching it, but what about those who actually knew us? And how many people who lived locally would see it? In fact, I remember feeling quite sick when the show started. I hadn't looked to see who was doing the voice-over, but as soon as I heard her, I knew it was Caroline Aherne – you'd recognise her voice anywhere.

'Imagine while you watched TV, it was watching you. What would you see?' she asked, before members of the cast were introduced to the viewing public. 'In Liverpool, Leon and June have been married for 52 years,' added Caroline as we flashed on and off almost immediately during the programme's opening sequence.

The first show that the producers had elected to kick the programme off was *Meteor Strike: Fireball From Space*, a Channel 4 documentary chronicling the descent of an asteroid that had crashed into the Urals in Russia the previous month. Even though the programme was based on real events and featured a certain amount of scientific analysis, it could have provided one of those end-of-the-world dramas with a viable plot.

'Bruce Willis will see to this!' observed Leon when he flashed up onscreen as the documentary showed the asteroid hurtling towards earth. It was a mildly amusing comment, I suppose, but it was just odd seeing Leon on TV, and even funnier to see me sitting next to him. Did I look uncomfortable? It was hard to tell during the space of such a brief clip.

The next time we appeared onscreen was when the programme turned its attention to an episode of *Embarrassing Bodies*, the Channel 4 show designed to debunk medical stigma but which always made me feel decidedly queasy. A shot of a man's inflamed scrotum popped up, followed by a shot of me covering my eyes. Onscreen, Leon turned to me and began to discuss food. 'Was that a low-calorie dinner tonight?' he asked. Then he promptly passed wind in front of the entire nation. How surreal – and how very rude!

As the show progressed, the opinions of the various cast members came to the fore, allowing the many different voices and personalities to emerge. The news of the Queen's gastroenteritis and her subsequent hospitalisation didn't seem to go down too well at all. Then came *Top Gear*'s two-part presenter, Jeremy Clarkson, offering an obvious focal point. 'He is stupid. Arrogant and insulting!'

proclaimed Leon, offering the first of many frank opinions that would define much of his time on the show.

Then, as we commented on a programme called *16 Kids and Counting* – which, as the title suggests, followed the travails of a family with 16 children – Leon's onscreen comments moved closer to home, as he started to discuss our Julie. 'The attention you had to give Julie because she wasn't well!' he began. 'She had bad eyes, she had terrible nosebleeds. What do you do if you've got 16 of them?' As Leon and I watched this back, we weren't sure what to think. I must admit though that I was quite relieved that Julie was down in New Zealand rather than in the UK and having to put up with a discussion of her previous ailments on national television.

As we watched the programme, I couldn't actually tell if my voice sounded funny. Of course, I thought it did – but did it? Really? Part of that nervousness went back to my school days, when I'd had elocution lessons. I'd had those because at school we'd done what was known as 'choral speaking' – which was where, in our drama group, we read out a dramatic passage – and I'd suffered cluttered speech (I spoke almost too quickly, my words crashing into each other), hence the lessons. As I watched myself on TV, I cast my mind back to those lessons and I remember thinking, 'You must remember to lower your voice for the next show.' Leon also sounded quite gruff in places. 'You need to clear your throat a bit more,' I told him at one point. He laughed and then, as if to confirm my anxiety, he turned around to me, pointed at the screen and said, 'Oh, your accent's come out, June!'

Then, Leon got agitated: 'I never said that!' he shouted. I can't quite remember which part of the show he was talking about but that was quite a strange moment because there he was, sitting in our living room, watching himself on TV and denying he had said something that had clearly been filmed. Before he could remonstrate any further, the show seemed to end. In fact, it had flown past, and there was a lot to take in – including the concept of the show itself and being introduced to all the other participating families onscreen.

'We weren't on it very much, were we?' he said as the credits rolled.

'Well, it's not the *Leon and June Show*, you know,' I replied.

In all honesty, neither of us was quite sure what to think. And so, we sat there in our lounge, having just watched ourselves watch TV – on TV – in that very same lounge. It all seemed quite surreal and there's no denying the fact that we both felt a little deflated.

'Oh, well,' I said, 'only three more episodes to go.'

* * *

The next morning Tania rang to congratulate us on our first appearance on the programme. She told us she was pleased with how everything had gone. The show itself had been well received by the general public and the broadcaster, Channel 4, also seemed happy with it.

'But we weren't on it enough, Tania!' said Leon, interrupting her thanks.

I think she found that quite funny and, of course, she became used to Leon's endless haranguing as the programme developed.

Soon after that call with Tania, the phone rang again. This time it was Leon's friend and bridge partner, Peter Amstrong. He'd been there at the bridge club on that fateful day when Leon had been 'discovered' by the show's researchers, and he'd watched the programme go out the previous evening. 'You weren't on it much, were you?' he said, much to Leon's irritation. When Leon went back to the bridge club five days later, on the following Tuesday, everyone was very complimentary though. Apparently, they'd all enjoyed watching the programme and Ivy, who ran the club and was Leon's mentor, congratulated him. He was very pleased about that, and that evening, he came back rather full of himself.

My brother Keith – who has always been supportive of everything I've ever done – also rang and told us he'd really enjoyed the show. 'I thought you were rather quiet, though, June,' he said. I wasn't really sure that was true, but I quickly realised what he was alluding to. Despite people's preconceptions – some of which have undoubtedly been based on our subsequent appearances on *Gogglebox* – Keith always felt that when it came to Leon and me, I was the bossy one. I'm not sure he was right, although he had grown up with me so maybe he was just getting his own back for all those years when I had clearly bossed him around!

In the brief period between the airing of the first episode and the filming of the second, nothing much else seemed to happen. We weren't sure whether we were really cut out to be television critics, but when the crew turned up for a second bout of filming, they told us not to worry too much about that. All we really needed to do was watch the programme we were shown and that was it. Spontaneity was what made everything work on the show and, as soon as we started normal conversations, we found that we could be ourselves.

Leon managed to take that to the extreme when, during the filming of the second episode, he demanded a snack. 'I'm bloody hungry!' he grumbled as we were midway through the shoot. In retrospect, that set a precedent quite early on for some of his subsequent behaviour. Thankfully, the production crew were very patient in dealing with us. I suppose it must have felt as if they were dealing with a petulant child, but they gave him a snack as if to pacify him. Of course, he would soon become known for his insufferable snacking!

The second episode was broadcast and, again, the reaction seemed very positive. I think it was after the transmission of the third show that we were told that *Gogglebox* had hit the million-viewer mark. To be honest, at the time I didn't really know whether that was meant to be any good or not: to me, it was meaningless. 'That must be good because think of what a million people looks like!' said Leon. 'But there's over eight million people in London alone,' I said. Of course, later, the show would attract nearly five million viewers, which was incredible, but during that first series, it seemed that people began to discover it by word-of-mouth.

One of our neighbours asked us very early on in that series how the programme itself worked. 'Were you told to say certain things? Do you have to learn lines?' they enquired. 'Have you ever tried to tell Leon to say something?' I replied. That comment alone was enough to make them understand that what they saw on *Gogglebox* was just us being us. I think the same thing was true of everyone else who appeared on the programme: they were just being themselves. In fact, that may have been why people started to watch the show.

Once we'd finished filming the four shows that made up that first series in March 2013, we didn't have any great expectations concerning any further shows. Anyway, we were due to go away to see Julie in New Zealand and when we came back, we thought that would be that. We got flowers and chocolates from the production team to thank us for our contribution. We also received a fee that went directly into Leon's account, never to be seen again! And then we headed off for a few weeks to New Zealand to see Julie, her husband Marc and our granddaughter Faye.

When we came back, we were the butt of a family joke. 'OK, that's all folks! You've had your hour of glory!' was the gist of what was being said. Maybe they were right, maybe it was time to get back to normal.

CHAPTER 15

· ·

'Yes, we'll do it!'

Gogglebox, Series 2

'*Y*es, we'll do it!' said Leon immediately when we got the call saying that *Gogglebox* was returning for a second series that would be due back on air in late September 2013. I don't think he even asked me about it. Then again, I felt lot more comfortable now that we'd done the first four shows, so I was happy for us to sign up for another series. The only difference was that this time we were signing up for 13 episodes rather than just four.

Once we'd started filming though, we were also aware that the show was as much to do with normal life as it was with what we actually said. If I had an accident in the kitchen while we were filming and Leon was sat in his chair, we didn't worry about it at all. Neither did the crew, they just kept on filming and the viewers simply heard the ensuing kerfuffle without ever actually knowing what had happened off-camera. In fact, throughout that series there was a sense of that wider life being introduced into the programme, sometimes with mixed results.

During one early episode in that series, we were introduced on the programme via a voiceover that mentioned our first date at the Silver Grill Café in Crewe, back in 1955. During another, I was filmed leafing through a TV guide when Leon began telling me a story – 'I went to the gents in Costa, unzipped my trousers and I couldn't find the hole in my underpants because I'd got them on back to front, so I had to pull the leg up before I could wee or I'd have done it on my trousers.' Of course, this, along with several other bits of detail, made it on to the show!

The way in which he badgered me to get him a Jacob's cream cracker became something of 'a moment' in itself, although I can't quite remember exactly when that actually happened. Maybe it stemmed back to that moment during those first four shows, but it was something the crew became increasingly accustomed to. Eventually, 'June, gerrusacracker!' became something of an odd catchphrase, so much so that when we'd go shopping, people would ask us if we were looking for the aisle where the crackers were located. Leon, in particular, found that most hilarious.

Some people we knew suggested that the show was an invasion of our privacy in some way, but it really wasn't. If you've got something important to discuss with your partner, you don't often do that while you're distracted by watching television. Our discussions as the camera rolled revolved around everyday chit-chat. We'd talk about silly things, really. I'd say things like, 'Did I see you buy some chocolates today, Leon?' And Leon, who was meant to be watching his weight, would squirm slightly as he tried to deny that he had. In hindsight, it's those small bits of people's lives that also endeared *Gogglebox* to the viewers because you felt that you were getting to know the cast. That's certainly how Leon and I felt about the other families or couples when we watched the programme.

The other thing we realised very quickly as we started filming again was the fact that we didn't have to be polite about everything that we watched. During the first four episodes we probably felt the need to be relatively polite. I had worried about that in particular because I thought if we referred to someone in a disparaging way, there might have been consequences – most specifically due to Leon's more colourful outbursts. Could you *really* call the Prime Minister a 'weak man' or openly state that he had 'big jowls now' while wondering whether he had dyed his hair? Could you really call UKIP's Nigel Farage a 'dickhead' and get away with it? Wasn't that slander? And, if so, wouldn't we simply get sued? Of course, there was no chance of that happening because there was a legal team who worked on the programme. Once again, though, I don't think it ever occurred to Leon to curb his opinion, regardless of the topic itself or who he was likely to upset. I think the viewers understood that quite quickly!

* * *

'I hate animals! All animals! Except cats,' barked Leon as we watched an episode of BBC TV's *Natural World*. It was October 2013 and probably five shows into the second series and we had been asked to watch an episode entitled 'Walrus: Two-Tonne Tusker'. There wasn't anything particularly contentious about that episode or even the walrus itself, who was essentially just trying to find a mate, but that didn't stop Leon's vitriolic outburst. And yet, his forthright attitude is probably what endeared him to so many people, who laughed along with his outbursts and, in some cases, nodded along in agreement with him.

The programmes Leon took real exception to were those where he felt the public was being ridiculed, most specifically talent shows. He thought that aspects of certain shows were expressly designed to make people look foolish in front of an audience of millions. During that second series of *Gogglebox*, *The X Factor* was one of the shows we watched and, of course, it was entertaining. During those early auditions, however, there were contestants who were truly hopeless. Of course, we laughed at these people but there was a simple question that lay at the heart of all of this: were we laughing *with* them or *at* them? It became something of a moral debate in our house. I read a piece in the paper that seemed to suggest that such shows were now a necessary outlet for new talent. We weren't entirely sure whether that was true or not. In the end we came to the conclusion that if somebody wanted their five minutes of fame, then so be it. They just needed to realise that they were going to get flack for it too. Ironically, we realised that also applied to us!

Of course, not everyone agreed with our opinions, especially when it came to politics. Every time Leon saw David Cameron appear on television the words 'posh boy' (or worse!) would spring from his mouth. On that occasion when he labelled Nigel Farage a 'dickhead' it seemed as if everybody in Liverpool agreed with him. 'You're dead right!' they'd say as they stopped us in the street to shake Leon's hand. But it wasn't just watching endless news footage of Cameron or Farage that solicited an angry reaction from Leon; it was the fact that the political world as a whole appeared to have lost touch with real life that bothered him. It bothered us both, in fact.

Both he and I felt that a lot of people who were making political decisions had led such narrow, sheltered lives they almost had no means of understanding the consequences of their policies. I wanted to say to them, 'Come to the supermarket with me! Come shopping with me and see how ordinary people behave when they shop these days!' Leon would have put it slightly differently: 'Come to the match with me and hear what people are really saying! Listen to what they want and need, what they're really worried about!' It amounted to the same thing.

If members of the political class dared venture out into the real world, or to our local supermarket, then they would see what we saw: people looking at the price of food and worrying about whether they could afford to buy their weekly shop. If they'd looked a bit deeper into that situation, they would also have seen the arrival of food banks, and they may have even understood the increasing need for them. In fact, there were people turning up at The Trussell Trust Food Bank – of which there are three in Liverpool – with printed signs itemising exactly what they needed. Such things made you realise that while we're living in the 21st century, in some respects, we appear to have gone back to the 1930s. We found that idea heartbreaking. It was probably some of that indignation that, alongside the more comedic moments that made it onto the programme, informed some of Leon's more outlandish comments.

Without wishing to sound too sanctimonious, by Series Two, we'd realised the cast were able to express genuine opinions that mattered. It was quite flattering for us, and for everyone who appeared on the show, to see that our views were being taken seriously in all sorts of different ways. Up until that point there really wasn't a show on television that allowed ordinary people to have a voice – *Gogglebox* changed that. For the first time you had people who were part of the TV-watching audience criticising what they were being shown. We were actually able to say, 'Why is this programme on television? It's rubbish!' Up until then, there had only been programmes like the BBC's *Points of View* and that wasn't quite the same. This show was about ordinary people sitting in their front rooms saying exactly what they wanted to say without a filter about any subject that was placed before them.

There was a wide variety of people, too, and it's that dynamic that makes the programme what it is. People were able to express their views, some more vociferously than others, and those watching the show were able to identify with that, too. That was quite revolutionary when you think about it because *Gogglebox*, for all its humorous moments, is also a programme that doesn't seem to be afraid to tackle the real issues – it just does it through the voice of ordinary people. I think that is why it's been so successful.

Most significant of all, though, the show has been successful because it is so often warm and positive. It also deals with real emotions. Certainly, people felt the latter in terms of certain instances that involved Leon and me. There was one moment in particular from Series Five in 2015 that seemed to capture viewers' imaginations as we watched Ridley Scott's epic movie from the year 2000, *Gladiator*.

'In Rome, I'd have been Leonidas the First!' proclaimed Leon as we began watching it.

'And the last!' I laughed.

'You would've been a beautiful slave girl, Juney!' he chortled.

Of course, the film wound its way to the closing scene, where the protagonist, Roman general Maximus Decimus Meridius (played by Russell Crowe) defeats Commodus, the treacherous new emperor (Joaquin Phoenix), in the Coliseum. Meridius, however, is mortally wounded and, as he dies, he appears to leave his earthly body to be reunited in the afterlife with his wife and child – themselves previously slain by Commodus' men.

As we watched this footage, I could sense Leon becoming increasingly emotional. 'I'd like to think that's true,' he said on the subject of the afterlife. 'Especially at our age,'

I added. Up until that point and despite our advancing years, Leon had refused to discuss death and yet here he was, doing it in the most public way imaginable.

'I'll join you. You'll see. Always, June,' he said, as we both wiped away our tears.

CHAPTER 16

Recognition and a Trip to the BAFTAs

'Where's Leon?' asked this voice I didn't recognise. I looked up from my breakfast to see a woman who was about 40-ish and athletic-looking standing by my table. I had no idea who she was. One of Leon's bridge partners perhaps? But what would she be doing here, down in London?

'He's getting a cooked breakfast,' I replied, unsure of what else to say.

'Oh, yes. He likes his food, doesn't he?' she smiled. 'I'll pop back to try and catch him.'

And with that, she walked off. A few minutes later, Leon came back and sat down with his plate laden. It was November 2014, and we had come down to London to watch the tennis at The O2 Arena. We had decided to stay in a hotel close to the venue itself, down in south London, rather than trog about town and, as far as Leon was concerned, a stay in a hotel was always a good excuse

• • • • • •

for a fry-up. As he began eating, I mentioned the woman who'd stopped by our table.

'June, I have no idea who you're talking about,' he said, between mouthfuls.

Suddenly, she reappeared and threw her arm around him.

'Hello! How are you, Leon?'

He looked at her in sheer astonishment.

'Sorry?' he spluttered. 'Who are you?'

'Oh, I've just seen you on television,' she replied. 'And I'm a big fan of yours.'

Leon looked bewildered, as did I. We had had people come up to us at different times while we were in Liverpool to discuss the programme, but this was slightly different. Here we were in London in a pretty busy hotel and here was someone who wanted to talk to us because she thought we were 'famous'! Neither of us quite knew what to do, but the young woman was very civil.

'I'll be back in a minute,' she said. She ran off only to come back almost immediately with her friend. When she returned, she asked Leon whether he'd take a photograph with her and her friend, and of course he willingly agreed. She told us she was a bodybuilder and that there was a convention going on at the hotel, but meeting us was a highlight of her stay. That evening, when we got back to the hotel after watching the tennis, she introduced us to a number of her colleagues, all of whom wanted photos, too. We posed for them but we were very tired so we sloped off to our room.

Our stint at The O2 had gone smoothly, and no one had recognised us in the slightest. Going shopping the next morning, however, was a different story. We'd been stopped on a number of occasions. It also happened as we caught the train from Euston back to Liverpool Lime Street. It all felt rather alien to us both. 'We'll just act as if this is normal,' said Leon.

Then, a couple of weeks later, we were shopping locally on Allerton Road at our local grocer's and bread shop when two teenagers stopped us and asked if they could have a selfie.

'Why do you want to have your photo taken with us?' asked Leon, rather bluntly.

'Because you're TV stars!' replied one. That sounded utterly ridiculous to us and, on the way home, we laughed at the very idea.

* * *

The year 2014 was the year when *Gogglebox* really broke through into the mainstream consciousness. The third series was filmed and began broadcasting in March, followed by a fourth in September. The viewing figures were doing remarkably well and had risen from over two million during Series Two in September 2013 to over four million the following year. We were happy to hear that because it meant that people were really enjoying the programme.

On a personal level, we noticed that more people stopped us in the street to have a chat and that generally this didn't bother us at all. They were mostly incredibly positive, and they wanted to discuss moments they'd seen on the show. Some people enjoyed the humour, others took things a bit more seriously. Overall, it made me realise just how much viewers had begun to identify with the programme and with the cast in general.

The recognition that the show had received was also being marked with its nomination at certain award shows, including the BAFTA Television Awards. As well as being nominated in the Reality and Constructed Factual category, the show was also in the running for the Radio Times Audience Award, a category voted for by the public. Tania Alexander rang us one March afternoon and told us that in order to canvas votes, she wanted us to appear on *The One Show*, BBC1's early-evening programme. We were utterly terrified at the prospect until she explained that we didn't have to go to *The One Show*'s studio, they would send a team to film us at home. It would be as if we were filming *Gogglebox*, in fact. Reassured by what she said, we agreed to appear on the programme.

Up until that point all of the filming we had done had been quite discreet. This, however, was different. On the appointed day, a huge truck emblazoned with a BBC logo parked outside our house, making it rather obvious what was going on. All the kids in the neighbourhood seemed excited by this and they sped up and down our road on their bikes. While we were in our front room waiting to be filmed, we realised that some of the cast from *Educating Yorkshire* – one of the other nominated shows and a programme we loved – were actually in *The One Show* studio, pitching for votes too. That put a certain amount of pressure on us. Lucy Whelan, one of the *Gogglebox* field producers, tried to reassure us, as did Tania. 'Just let the audience know what's unique about *Gogglebox*,' she said. That seemed easy enough.

As *The One Show* crew set up, I grew increasingly tense.

'What are you going to say?' I asked Leon.

'I don't know, but I'll think of something,' he replied.

That worried me even more. But soon, the cameras were ready to roll and we were being told that we needed to be ready at any minute.

'You tell them about the show because I'm only going to say one thing,' said Leon. I had no idea what he meant but there wasn't much more time to think as we had started filming.

'Basically, our show represents the real opinions of the general public, so you really should vote for us,' I said. Or something to that effect. Then, I paused and waited for Leon to pick up the baton.

'Yes!' he added rather loudly. 'And if you vote for *Gogglebox*, then June will show you her knicks!'

It took a few seconds for what he'd said to sink in. I looked up and I could see the cameraman shaking with laughter behind the camera as I realised exactly what had just happened.

'Will that bit be edited out?' I asked in horror.

'No,' came the reply.

I was flabbergasted.

Tania rang shortly afterwards to thank us and to say she'd thought it was a brilliant attempt at winning votes. Leon, of course, was beside himself with glee.

In the end, it was hard to know whether we'd generated any votes whatsoever – although we were told we had – because the BBC's *Doctor Who* scooped that particular Audience award. But *Gogglebox* did win the BAFTA it was nominated for and we were very proud of that. A few months later, Tania visited us with the BAFTA itself and we were astounded by how heavy the trophy was.

Unfortunately, though, there was a knock-on effect from *The One Show* moment: whenever I went into town, I would be walking down the street and I'd hear people shouting after me: 'June, show us yer knicks!' It was, I suppose, some sort of compliment!

* * *

Two months before the BAFTAs took place, and just as we were about to film the third series, *Gogglebox* was nominated for a TRIC Award. The Television and Radio Industries Club was formed in the 1930s and their annual awards ceremony is a hugely prestigious event which takes place at The Grosvenor House Hotel in March of each year and is attended by some of the biggest names in TV. Executive producer Tania Alexander had very kindly asked us if we wanted to accompany her to the ceremony, and we were thrilled at the prospect.

We travelled down to London and checked into our hotel before heading to The Grosvenor House Hotel for the lunchtime awards ceremony. The hotel itself seemed rather quiet. Then Tania rang and asked us where we were. It was then that we realised we had used the wrong hotel entrance! Thankfully, she came and found us. 'Have you done your stint on the red carpet?' she asked. Of course we hadn't. And, for a split second, we were bemused as to why anyone would want us to walk down the red carpet. Nevertheless, we did, and we had our picture taken and were asked a few questions about other television shows. It all seemed rather surreal. Then, we went into the ballroom at the hotel and that felt even more remarkable.

'What does a man have to do to get a glass of champagne around here?' asked a voice as we arrived at our designated table. We had no idea who the man was asking the question. 'Oh, hello, I'm Stephen,' he said, introducing himself. Again, we were none the wiser until Tania pointed out that he was actually the man who not only runs but owns Studio Lambert – the company that makes *Gogglebox*.

As we were talking to Tania and Stephen we saw a number of famous faces milling around. The comedian Keith Lemon was sitting at the table behind us. 'Look at that dickhead!' said Leon, without even having met the man. Again, I was slightly mortified. Peter André, the Australian pop star, walked over to us. 'My dad and I love the show!' he said, rather enthusiastically. He seemed like a very nice chap and I was relieved when he escaped any kind of uncharitable comments from Leon. Then, Tania mentioned that if *Gogglebox* won the award, she wanted us to pick it up. We genuinely didn't know what to say – we thought we'd just popped down to London for a good day out, but this was completely different!

Nervous and excited, we sat down and waited for the awards ceremony to start. Then came the moment when the winner of the Best Entertainment category was due to be announced: 'And the winner is ... *Gogglebox*!' We were sat fairly near the stage but walking up to collect the award seemed to take forever. Leon's mobility wasn't great either and he doesn't like stairs or heights, so things were slightly tricky.

As we walked up with Tania and Stephen, my heart was pounding in my chest. I suddenly thought to myself, 'I've seen people on television doing this and now it's me doing it!' I really felt as though I was standing outside of myself, watching myself. It was as if I was dreaming, or in some sort of bubble. I was trusting Leon to come up with something as we simply hadn't prepared anything. I could tell he was excited, but for once, he also seemed rather overwhelmed. He came up with a joke that was rather dated and doesn't bear repeating here. But Leon had a stage and so he made the most of it, soliciting applause and laughter in equal measure. Then, as we were having our photo taken backstage, Leon met *This Morning*'s Eamonn Holmes, who had also won an award. He told us how much he enjoyed watching *Gogglebox* before he and Leon lapsed into 'footy-speak'. While I watched the two of them talk to each other with ease, I felt a sense of disbelief and genuine pride.

CHAPTER 17

Life Away from
the Cameras

The success of *Gogglebox* has been quite astonishing. As a result, we received some wonderful invitations to attend various functions since we started filming, back in 2013, and, quite often, accepted them. One of my earliest memories of one of those occasions dates back to the summer of 2014, just as the show was really starting to become successful. For some reason or another, we were invited to a Labour Party fundraiser at The Roundhouse in Chalk Farm, north London. By that point Ed Miliband had become leader of the Party, and even though Leon preferred his brother, David, we decided to go because we were down in London for a short visit.

We arrived and there seemed to be a distinct absence of MPs, but we found hundreds of party workers milling around. However, Hilary Benn, who was shadow secretary of state for communities and local government at the time, came over and asked who we were. We told him and Leon asked where everyone was. 'Oh, they've gone to pre-drinks,' he answered. 'Pre-drinks?' replied Leon. 'The Labour Party's becoming more like the Tory Party by the minute!' I looked at Hilary Benn, but I couldn't tell what he made of that comment, although Leon was chuckling away.

As we left Hilary Benn in peace, Leon popped to the gents. On the way back, he ran into Stephen Fry, who was hosting the event. 'I've just met a friend of yours!' he smiled when he got back to the table where we were sitting. Of course, I had never met Stephen, but I had watched most of the programmes he's been in down the years, so Leon suggested we go over and talk to him. I felt embarrassed about doing that, but of course that didn't stop Leon.

'Excuse me, Mr Fry, may I introduce my wife, June? She's a great fan of yours and has been since the days of *Jeeves and Wooster*,' he said. Stephen Fry smiled and asked me where I was from so I told him that, although I had lived in Liverpool for most of my life, I was originally from South Wales. He asked if I lived near Cardiff. I said I didn't, but I lived not too far away. He then went on to say, 'I'm a Fellow of Cardiff University.' I told him that my granddaughter was deliberating between studying at Cardiff and Liverpool. He smiled and laughingly said, 'Oh, Cardiff is really the only choice!' before adding that it was really a very good university.

When he realised I was from Tredegar, he asked if Neil Kinnock had been my MP. I said, 'No, he was Member of Parliament for Bedwellty, a neighbouring constituency.'

'Of course!' he said. 'How silly of me.'

Then, Leon said he was a great *Blackadder* fan, to which Stephen Fry smiled and then switched the conversation to Liverpool. Although we only spoke for a few minutes, he was just as I imagined him to be: charming, polite and a great conversationalist.

During the rest of the evening, we did see a number of people that we recognised, including a number of MPs. At one point, Neil Kinnock walked past and, again, Leon suggested I should talk to him. When I refused, he intervened once more. 'Neil, Neil! There's someone from Tredegar here!' he shouted rather loudly. To his credit, Neil Kinnock was over like a shot. 'Where exactly are you from?' he asked. 'Ashvale,' I replied. 'Ah! I know it very well because I'm from Ashvale, too!' he said. 'I know you are,' I told him. 'You're the same age as my brother, Keith, and your mother used to come into our house because she was the district nurse.'

After that, we chatted about our days in Trede-gar before being called to order as we were asked to sit down for dinner. Once people had seen us talking to Neil Kinnock, however, all sorts of people came over during the course of the evening, including Tristram Hunt, who was shadow education minister at the time. Typically, Leon told him that if Labour got in during the 2015 election, then they should scrap university tuition fees. In fact, after an evening of talking to a number of MPs, Leon seemed most pleased with himself. 'See! I *do* know people in high places!' he laughed as we left. It had been another good night out and, again, it is quite bizarre to think we'd mingled in such exalted company.

* * *

Appearing on *Gogglebox* also led to some rather amusing situations in our everyday lives. When people recognised us in Tesco's, they said things like, 'Don't you have someone to do your shopping for you?' That's very funny. And when people saw we were driving a car that was 14 years old, they tended to ask why we hadn't bought a new, flashier model. The truth was, we didn't use the car very often. In fact, we took the bus into town quite often and that usually led to a conversation that started as follows:

'Aren't you from *Gogglebox*? What are you doing on *this* bus?'

People did think that we really led a strange life when we told them we actually lived in the same house we'd always lived in and our life really was quite ordinary.

Of course, since we started filming, we embraced social media. Leon was given an iPad by the *Gogglebox* team for his 80th birthday, and Scott McKee (our cameraman) and Rory McGariggle (our soundman) helped us get set up on Twitter. They explained how it worked while we had a cup of tea and from thereon in, I took care of our account. I'd heard all about Twitter and how Stephen Fry had a love-hate relationship with it, but it was interesting to see how it actually worked. Once we'd got set up in November 2013, certain people tweeted us, I answered, and the next thing we knew, we had a few thousand followers. I realised quite quickly that when you put something out there, you really have to think about what you're going to say, and it's important to be positive. All in all, Twitter kept us in contact with the wider world.

As well as engaging in the world through social media, we were also invited to various other places, including Old Trafford, where Leon went to watch the cricket from the new stand a few years ago. He was really thrilled by that. I've also been invited to the Empire theatre in Liverpool on a number of occasions, a theatre we visited in our early years in the city and where we subsequently took our grandchildren to see various pantomimes. But I think the most surreal moment we enjoyed during our filming of *Gogglebox* was the moment when we became the prize in a charity auction for Age Concern. The prize itself consisted of having afternoon tea with Leon and I at The Hilton in Liverpool.

In the end, somebody bid £6,000 to have afternoon tea with us. We couldn't believe that! The two young women who came along were delighted to meet us. It turned out it was their boss who placed the bid. He works in France but he'd heard a lot about us because of the show, so he put the bid in and then got them to come along in his place. I think they enjoyed the afternoon and, after we had finished eating and were about to leave, the head waiter said he'd been asked if we would have our photograph taken with a couple who were having their wedding reception at the hotel. It appeared the bride's father had recognised us and the family were great *Gogglebox* fans, so we were happy to oblige.

Even prior to appearing on *Gogglebox* charity had always been something we cared about and there were times when we were able to get involved in various projects. Every Christmas Leon and I always made sure that we'd make a donation to a local charity, and then we'd select a second charity too. One of those charities was FOMO Malawi, an organisation that cares for thousands of orphaned children in Malawi itself. It was brought to my attention via Twitter by Brendan Rendall, an incredible

man who, at the time of writing, is engaged in a 4,000-kilo-
metre coast-to-coast African run to raise money for school
accommodation, having already successfully completed
runs to raise funds for a science block and accommodation for girls. He visited us in 2017 to show us footage of
the school building and the children who attend it. Being
able to help him and that organisation has been another
positive thing to come out of the show, and I have kept in
touch with him following Leon's passing.

Of course, one of the biggest things that *Gogglebox*
has managed to contribute to since it has been on air is
the Stand Up to Cancer campaign. It involves a special
episode of the show being filmed with the regular cast,
as well as genuine celebrities like Naomi Campbell, Kate
Moss, Ozzy and Sharon Osbourne, and Freddie Flintoff,
and that episode is then included in Channel 4's evening of
programming in support of the charity. Watching the footage of those affected by cancer battling the disease is truly
heartbreaking, but we hope that episode makes a difference and gets people to donate.

Gogglebox viewers may also remember the episode of
the programme where Leon attempted to make his own
charitable donation to BBC Children in Need, although
they may remember that for all the wrong reasons! As
I've said previously, Bernicoff is quite a unique name and

viewers may recall that the automated voice recognition system used by the charity's phoneline had a slight issue with understanding Leon when he rang in. I think it was probably after his third attempt at registering his name that he ended up screaming our surname into the receiver in a rather deranged manner: 'B-E-R-N-I-C-O-F-F! Double "F" for foxtrot!' Of course, once he'd made his donation, he turned around and proclaimed, 'I've just donated £30!' He seemed rather proud of that fact, until I reminded him that we were being filmed and now he looked like someone boasting about it all in front of the entire nation!

Leon and I were very proud to support Stand Up for Cancer and, of course, it was something that was very important to everyone involved in the programme in the wake of Caroline Aherne's passing from cancer in July 2016. We were on holiday in Portugal when the news broke. I was washing my hair in the bathroom.

'June! Come here now!' shouted Leon from the lounge.

I told him I was rather busy, but he insisted and when I walked out, he pointed at the TV screen where the British news was on, and where they were paying tribute to Caroline. That day, so many people came up to us in the street to offer their condolences that it almost seemed as if half of the country had moved to Portugal. It also shows how loved she was. We had never met Caroline or her co-narrator and friend, Craig Cash, but as with all the cast, crew and the rest of the country, we were deeply upset when she died. She was only 52, and she was so very talented, and so loved. Craig, of course, continues to narrate the show and he's kept that sense of comfort that she brought to the programme alive through his own wonderful delivery.

* * *

When we weren't filming *Gogglebox*, Leon and I did watch lots of 'great telly' – to quote the opening line of the programme. We enjoyed period dramas, as well as soaps like *Emmerdale* and *Coronation Street*, and classic comedy, like *The Morecambe & Wise Show*. Leon loved *Frasier*, along with a good Western, while I enjoyed shows like *Pointless*, *24 Hours In A&E* and, my guilty pleasure, *First Dates*. Once we started appearing on *Gogglebox*, though, we did end up watching television shows in a more critical manner, which I suppose was to be expected.

During the ten series that we filmed, we also found that the programme gave a certain structure to our lives. There were simple day-to-day elements that we had to accommodate. For instance, we knew that going out might take us a bit longer than usual because somebody would probably want to talk to us about the programme.

On a more practical level, though, we also had to orga-nise our social lives around the filming itself. We were quite happy to do that too because, by the time we were filming the likes of Series Seven in 2016, we weren't going out that much in the evenings anyway. The fact that the series had expanded to a 15-week run also meant that during the filming period we'd say to our friends and family that we couldn't commit to doing things at the weekend. Of course, we also organised our holidays around the filming schedule.

It's unfair to describe our appearance on *Gogglebox* as work per se because we never considered it in those terms. But, as you get older, you do need to do things regularly to give a certain shape to your life. It keeps you active and alert, otherwise you can become very lazy. Having a sense of order in life and certain goals based around film-ing proved to be very important to us, especially Leon, because his health had begun to deteriorate during the previous three years. In fact, he looked forward to filming and I think in a number of respects it kept him going right up until the end of his life.

As well as making time to film, Leon and I were also adamant that we had to maintain our other interests. In Leon's case that meant playing bridge every Tuesday and Thursday afternoon. Meanwhile, I did Tai Chi every

Monday morning and went swimming every Tuesday and Thursday morning. Staying active in that way was really important to me, and it still is.

Away from the cameras too, we were close to the *Gogglebox* team who worked with us, including Harriet Manby, who manages the cast, and Lucy Whelan and Vic Ray, who produced our shoots at different times. At one point in September 2013, my brother Keith was very ill and he ended up in hospital. Tania Alexander was very understanding and rang to tell us that we shouldn't film that week, but I felt we had to. There was nothing in the programmes that we were asked to watch that was in any way sensitive, but I did feel emotional about almost anything we had to watch. Equally, I also really wanted to make sure that we fulfilled our commitment for that week.

After we'd finished filming that Friday's programme we travelled to Cardiff to see Keith and we were recognised soon after arriving at the hospital and then again on the ward. Keith was surprised to see us and greeted us by saying, 'Aren't you meant to be filming?' Then he added, 'Everybody on the ward's looking at you because they've seen you on television!' I told him to be quiet and tried to find out what was wrong with him, but in a way that whole episode underlines just how central filming was to our lives. If you were in the normal working world and things went wrong, you just had to deal with it – it was the same with us when it came to filming.

Leon and I also enjoyed hearing stories about the crew and their families. There was one particular incident involving Vic Ray, who had to produce a shoot on Mother's Day. It meant she wasn't able to spend the day with her own mother or her young son, who was up in Bakewell, Yorkshire. Leon was rather put out about this so he insisted we take her for lunch at a bar and grill in town, near the hotel where the crew were staying.

'You've got have a champagne cocktail on Mother's Day, Vic!' he announced as we sat down to eat. Vic and I did indeed have *one* champagne cocktail while Leon enjoyed a couple more and a three-course meal. When we got back to the shoot that afternoon he kept falling asleep! As usual, I was mortified by this and I was concerned that we'd all get into trouble over the whole episode. The crew, who'd all been present at Leon's insistence, seemed to find it amusing, particularly Rory and Scott. I suppose it was Leon being Leon once again!

CHAPTER 18

The Final Series

Hindsight is a wonderful thing, but sometimes when I think back, I am not entirely sure what it was that endeared us to the *Gogglebox* viewers. Did they just find us funny? Was it Leon's colourful use of language? Was it simply the fact that I told him off constantly for misbehaving? Or was it the fact that he was capable of saying things that others only dared to think? It's hard to tell. In all honesty, we didn't discuss it that much but it was probably all of those things combined.

One question that we did get asked quite often, though, was how we'd managed to stay together for so long. After all, we were married for 57 years, so that was quite an achievement. 'Were there moments where you felt like walking out?' certain people asked us. Leon had a good answer for that question: 'Yes, I did walk out, but she just didn't notice. Probably because it was a Friday night and I was home by the early hours of Saturday!' What he omitted to say was that it was his weekly boys' night out and he'd gone to the pub and was back at his usual time!

If we were discussing relationships in a serious manner with someone, though, Leon was far less flippant. He'd often point out that we'd got married with a certain amount of difficulty, so the idea of throwing that away never entered his head. In fact, immediately after we married he'd turned to me and said, 'Now I can look after you.' And he really meant that. In fact, when he fell ill – and I'm not sure either of us realised just how ill he really was – he turned to me and, in one of his quieter moments, said, 'Thank you for looking after me.'

Despite Leon's undoubted brashness, and the fact that he liked to turn everything into a joke, he really believed that in this life you had to care for people. He cared for his parents, his two aunts and, in later life when she came to stay with us, my mother (who, in her late eighties, was not only deaf but had lost her sight too), as well as the rest of our family. The caring side to his personality was also what endeared him to his students and work colleagues for whom he was always willing to go the extra mile. Quite literally, in certain cases …

One of the letters I received when he passed away was from a teacher who lived not too far from us when she started working. She had had to get three buses to school, meaning she had to get up at a ridiculously early hour. When Leon found this out, he arranged to make a small detour to pick her up in his car and take her to school so that she could have a bit of a lie-in. Of course, Leon joked that it meant he always had a young woman in the car with him! It was, according to him, 'very flattering'. But, of course, his boasting masked the care with which he'd reacted to the situation, and it also underlined how comfortable he was around women.

In fact, Leon would often boast that he and I had invented sexual equality a long time before feminism passed into the modern vocabulary. This extravagant claim was based on the simple fact that, despite getting married, not only had we continued to have individual bank accounts but we had different banks too! Obviously, we knew who had what in what account, but we also had that little bit of independence that is so important in a relationship. We did a lot together, but we did lots on our own too, and made sure that we had our own interests.

When Helen and Julie arrived, I went to night school and did dressmaking so I could make them clothes, just as my mother had always made mine. I'd go to the occasional concert at the Philharmonic while Leon babysat, and then the next week, if he went to football, it would be the other way round. Then, when we saw each other that evening, we would regale each other with what we'd done during the day. We always took a real interest in what had happened while we'd been apart. I think there are a lot of people who drift apart because they don't talk to each other properly and they end up with very little in common. Equally, you have to be interested in people other than just your partner, otherwise things become very dull. Your friends are important, and your interest in them helps keep your own relationship alive because it allows you to talk about a wider circle of people, and about life in general as a result.

* * *

Leon turned 80 in October 2014. We waited until after New Year in order to have a big party that Julie and her family could attend, and on 2nd January, we hired out the Joe Mercer Suite at Goodison Park to celebrate properly. Leon loved it, and the *Liverpool Echo* presented him with a one-off front page commemorating his birthday.

Unfortunately, shortly after that party, Leon went into hospital and his health began to deteriorate. The problems he had seemed to recur and he had to go back to hospital on three occasions. Leon being Leon meant that he was determined not to let illness get in the way of what he wanted to do.

That said, when we started filming the tenth series of *Gogglebox* in early September 2017, he didn't seem himself. As the series progressed, I felt increasingly worried about him. As we finished up one particular shoot, I asked him if he felt tired. He told me that he did and we agreed to take a brief three-week break from filming. During that period, we went to Helen's for a few days as both Frances and Sam were home from university and we could all go out for a meal to celebrate Leon's birthday.

On our return home, Leon began to reminisce about our children's childhood, and how we had visited South Wales every holiday so my parents could spend as much time as possible with their grandchildren. He spoke of how we kept them amused on the four-hour car journeys, only to be asked after half an hour or so, 'Are we nearly to Nana's yet?' Of course, as ever, Leon's memories revolved around food: 'The smell of your mother's meat and potato pies baking when we arrived always made that long journey very worthwhile!' he laughed.

Come the following shoot for the penultimate show, however, he told me he felt great again, and he wanted to carry on. In fact, he genuinely did seem back on form. As we watched a news package covering the allegations concerning pornography found on Conservative MP Damian Green's laptop, I could hear Leon chuckling.

'I do believe people are being named and shamed and sometimes they are innocent,' I commented.

'You're never innocent if you're a Tory!' Leon fired back in his customary sharp-tongued manner. Then his softer side came to the fore as we watched an episode of *Strictly Come Dancing*, which featured a particularly impressive performance by singer Alexandra Burke and her partner, Gorka Marquez, who danced their way through 'Supercalifragilisticexpialidocious', the famous song from *Mary Poppins*.

'Makes you want to dance, doesn't it?' he smiled.

On Sunday, 10th December, we filmed footage for what was due to be the final episode of the series to be broadcast five days later. Despite my reservations about his health, Leon insisted we go ahead with the filming. Once again, he seemed to struggle through it all and I sensed things really weren't quite right. After the filming had ended, I said to him that this was probably it, and that we should stop contributing to the show now. He sat there with his Christmas jumper on, but he was quiet and I could tell he was sad. He made no comment whatsoever about stopping filming and then, the next day, on the Monday, he woke up and he said, 'I'm going to ring Tania after Christmas and tell her that we're definitely up for filming the next series!'

That day, we had planned to finish our Christmas shopping and go out for lunch, but it was so very cold and wet we decided against it. Leon reminded me he had bought all his presents the previous week but we still needed to buy food in case the weather was too bad to travel. However, Elspeth Joyce, a very old friend and neighbour who we always saw regularly, called round and spent the afternoon with us. We discussed our Christmas plans as she was spending the holidays away from home at her son's. Leon was in festive spirit and we decided to put the tree up the following day.

On the Tuesday morning, Leon said, 'I fancy a curry!' and so we prepared one. However, later on that day, I was a little concerned and, after much protesting from Leon, we finally went to the hospital. There, in spite of his insistence that he was fine, he underwent rigorous and thorough tests. He constantly asked to go home, as he was hungry. Eventually, the results of all his tests came back: they were all normal and he was told he could indeed go home by the doctor in charge. Needless to say, I was told there and then by Leon what a waste of time it had been when he knew all along that he was all right and there were people waiting to be seen who needed treatment far more than he did! As we left the hospital, he thanked the doctor and then proceeded to wish staff and patients in A&E a merry Christmas. On the way home, he chatted away endlessly. Our taxi driver was from Albania, so he wanted to know all about where the man was from and what his children were up to.

When we got home, Leon enjoyed his curry, and over our meal, we opened some Christmas cards that had arrived. This prompted more tales of Christmases past. There was one particular festive period that he recalled where, as a child, Julie had suffered very severe nosebleeds in the week leading up to Christmas. As usual, we spent Christmas in South Wales that year, and we all went to Abergavenny Market, where Julie was asked to select the turkey. 'Can we have that one with the red ribbon, Nana?' she asked, pointing to the prizewinning turkey that was simply huge. Of course, my parents bought it. Then, when they got home, with the bird in hand, came the problem of cooking it! We both laughed about that.

'I think I'll ring her now and remind her of it,' said Leon, not thinking of the 12-hour time difference between the UK and New Zealand, nor the fact that Julie would be at work.

At about 10:30pm, he said he was going to bed. I asked if he was sure he was all right, but he just got up out of his chair and went upstairs. I told him I'd clear up and be up very soon. 'I'll be asleep by then, in my own bed,' he said, and when I went up, he was. The next morning, we called the ambulance and he was admitted to hospital for one last time.

* * *

'No weeping and wailing over me, Junc! No weeping and wailing, none of that!' Leon had said to me on a rare occasion when we were talking about death. Despite our advanced years, he never wanted to discuss the subject. In fact, he would often change the subject when it was brought up, but he was also clear that he hated the idea of the solemnity that surrounds death itself. I tried to remember that when he passed away on 23rd December 2017, but it wasn't that easy. Death never is because the world carries on regardless of your loss, and you are sat there wondering what to do.

Leon passed away following a short illness that in the end resulted in him contracting pneumonia and sepsis. While Helen, Julie and I were still in shock at the hospital, the news of Leon's passing had made it on to social media. I only found out because somebody sent me a text saying: 'Please tell me what I've read about Leon isn't right.' Apparently, someone had posted something on Facebook. I wasn't on Facebook so I couldn't see what had been said, and none of us were quite sure what to do. I texted *Gogglebox* cast manager Harriet Manby and she had read the same post. She and I discussed what to do, and once she'd had a conversation with Tania Alexander, they kindly agreed to issue a statement on our behalf in a bid to give us a modicum of privacy.

Tania wrote the statement itself and sent it to me to check. Then, at 5pm, it went out to the press and media. Tania had also warned me that the BBC *Ten O'clock News* were going to report Leon's death. The girls and I debated whether we should even watch it. In the end, we couldn't bring ourselves to do that but my brother Keith did ring me. 'Just imagine if Leon was watching the news! He'd be incredulous,' he said in a bid to cheer me up. In black and white, that may appear insensitive, but it wasn't meant that way in the slightest, and I did chuckle at the thought.

The following day, on 24th December, the *Gogglebox Christmas Special* aired on Channel 4. Of course, the production team hadn't had time to make a change to the programme but they had managed to get the channel to add a nice tribute at the start that dedicated the episode to Leon's memory. The episode itself opened with a piece of footage of Leon. He was sitting in his usual armchair, with a box of Quality Street in his lap, which he was meant to wrap.

'June! Come and tie this!' he shouted to me. I was in the kitchen. As a result, I didn't see him open the tin, take out a sweet, unwrap it, pop it in his mouth and then throw

the wrapper back in the tin before putting the lid back on.
Then, he started to wrap the box before the show's familiar theme tune kicked in. Thinking back, it was a good
final scene.

* * *

The outpouring of kindness from the general public that
met Leon's passing was genuinely quite remarkable. Ironically, the only person who wasn't there to bask in all the
attention was Leon himself. I am sure he would have been
astonished, overwhelmed and quite proud. A lot of people
who watch the show have come up to me since his death
and have said, 'I don't wish to intrude, but I just want to say
sorry about Leon.' And I do find it comforting, although
that's not quite the right word, because of course there is
sadness in all of this. But there is also genuine warmth in
people's sentiments. I think that it's really nice that they feel
bothered enough to say that we have touched their lives in
some way – something that, to me, still seems quite strange.

Prior to Leon's passing, we hadn't discussed funeral
arrangements. Leon would just say, 'You'll know what to
do, June. I'll leave it to you.' Despite this, he had made
it clear that he wanted his funeral to be a celebration of
his life rather than a mournful affair – 'I want everybody
there, but I don't want them dressed in black, and I want it

lively too!' he once said. In fact, it really was rather lively and, despite the obvious sadness involved, the celebratory aspect was what I really wanted to emphasise.

The ceremony itself was held at Springwood Crematorium on 3rd January 2018, and many people from all the different areas of our lives turned up to pay their respects. I was incredibly nervous about speaking, but an old teaching colleague of mine came round and said, 'June, just think of it as if you're taking Assembly.' It was a good piece of advice. Faced with arranging a funeral, you really do need as much advice as you can get because there are times when you feel somewhat lost. Helen, Julie and I discussed everything and made all the necessary arrangements as that was exactly what Leon would have wanted.

We chose the music that Leon liked, which, of course, included Frank Sinatra, so obviously we played 'My Way' – largely because he did do everything his way! We also felt that we had to play the theme tune to the BBC TV series, *Z Cars*, purely because Everton Football Club run on to the pitch with that playing over the Goodison Park tannoy at every home game. Of course, not everyone was aware of that on the day, so there were a number of puzzled expressions on assorted people's faces as the theme to a TV cop show that ceased transmitting in 1978 blared out. Finally, we played 'Lara's Theme' – better known as 'Somewhere My Love', or 'our tune' as we used to refer to it – taken from one of our favourite films of the sixties, *Doctor Zhivago*.

Leon had always described himself rather proudly as something of 'a bitter Blue', so Everton obviously did exert a certain presence over the service, with a number of attendees wearing the club's colours. I found it moving when a family friend, Simon – who had moved into the house opposite with his family when he was seven and was a huge Liverpool supporter – said he was coming. He'd been at Heysel, he was at Hillsborough, he'd been everywhere with Liverpool. But he still went and bought an Everton scarf for the funeral. 'Nobody will understand the significance of this apart from the Bernicoffs!' he said. In the end, he couldn't actually come to the service but the thought was there and he was willing to change his colours for the day, such was his affection for Leon. The funeral director understood just how important to Leon Everton had been too. Prior to the service, he had reminded me about Leon's Everton scarf, and I went to fetch that while Helen got his bobble hat. We placed them both on top of the coffin. A lot of people commented on that, saying it would have been exactly what Leon would have wanted.

The religious aspects of the service were a little more complicated to tackle. Initially, we'd approached a rabbi to conduct the service, but we decided that faith was just one aspect of Leon's life, and we felt he would have wanted a ceremony that was as inclusive as possible. As a result, the funeral director suggested we contact a celebrant instead. I didn't know what a celebrant was prior to that and for those of you who don't, it is basically a secular equivalent of a priest or rabbi.

In fact, the gentleman who officiated over the proceedings was not only an old boy from Gateacre, where we'd both taught, but also lived for a time at Strawberry Field, the children's home with which Leon had had such a strong connection, so it all seemed very appropriate. I wanted to insert the *Kaddish* – the Jewish prayer that Leon had recited when we'd visited Auschwitz – into the proceedings. I knew it was a religious element but I also felt it reflected Leon's culture and heritage, and so I included it as a mark of respect. Thankfully, the celebrant was a talented linguist and he was willing to learn how to read the *Kaddish* out in Hebrew. I was delighted when he agreed to do that and he was able to read it out towards the end of the service. Then, I felt worried in case his reading inadvertently upset anyone. Had Leon been there, he would have told me not to be so silly – 'If you want to do it, just do it!' is what he would have undoubtedly said. As a result, I realised that I was worrying about nothing. This was Leon's final day and I was determined to reflect who he truly was. The girls and I talked about it, and they felt the same way.

On the day itself, Julie spoke on behalf of Helen and herself. She began by pointing out that Helen had inherited Leon's kind and generous nature, his love of history and sport, accompanying him to so many Everton matches, while she herself shared his mischievousness and his sense of humour. Helen, she said, he put on a pedestal, but she was Leon's baby. Her earliest memories of life centred around the bedtime stories that Leon used to tell her and Helen, a firm favourite being his adaptation of a *Brer Rabbit* story, where Brer Rabbit ends up playing for Everton. Fouled by the wicked Brer Fox, playing for Liverpool, Brer Rabbit was given a penalty and scored the winning goal! Then came a multitude of memories of our family life. She spoke of the endless support Leon afforded her and Helen, and of the close bond that existed between him and his sons-in-law, Marc and Ian. 'Thankfully, neither of them supported Liverpool!' she quipped. She also spoke of the pride and encouragement that Leon offered our grandchildren and emphasised the sheer happiness we felt when we were altogether.

Once Julie had finished, Faye spoke, followed by Frances. Faye also recounted the joy of spending time with her grandfather, and the pride with which Leon watched her play tennis. She also spoke of his pride when she went to university, and his extremely generous nature, demonstrated just weeks before when she phoned to tell him she had passed her first-year exams. He had insisted Julie buy her a gift as a reward for passing them. Frances, meanwhile, recited Shakespeare's rumination on immortality, Sonnet 18, in a manner that was deeply affecting.

When it came to my turn to speak, I intended to talk for maybe three to five minutes. Once I had started, however, I think I may have got a bit carried away. I'm not quite sure how long I ended up speaking for, but it was quite a time, over 20 minutes or so. To be honest, there was just so much to say about Leon, and I wanted to say it one last time ...

CHAPTER 19

. . . .

Life After Leon

On the evening of Friday, 23rd February 2018, I poured myself a nice glass of red wine in the kitchen and then walked through into the lounge. Like millions of other viewers, I turned on the television to watch *Gogglebox*. Harriet Manby had told me that the show would be dedicated to Leon so I was ready for that. In fact, the show's end card read: 'In loving memory of Leon Bernicoff'. On a personal level, that was such a kind and thoughtful gesture and I really appreciated it.

If I get emotional about things, it's usually when I'm alone. People do say that I spend quite a lot of time on my own. That's because I like my own company, but sometimes it also just reminds me that Leon is no longer here with me. I did find that night, as I watched the programme, that I turned involuntarily to the chair to my left to say, 'Look, Leon, they've dedicated the show to you!' In fact, I pointed to the screen and almost started to speak the words themselves when I realised he wasn't there. Instead, I had a release of emotion at that point that I hadn't been able to have up until then. That was not a negative thing, quite the opposite. For me it was a positive reaction and, in a way, it really was the start of my grieving process.

Until that evening, emotionally speaking, I'd almost been in a peculiar vacuum. It's hard to explain exactly why and maybe it only makes sense to people who have experienced that kind of loss. Occasionally, I'd get upset, but I was never one of those people who met my friends and said things like, 'I've cried myself to sleep for nights.' It just wasn't like that for me, and Leon had always said to me that if he passed away before me, I had to stay positive, keep going and do anything that I wanted to do. I remembered that, and that is what I have done. Maybe I am an odd person, though, because that night, while watching the first episode of that 11th series, I felt I was finally able to start dealing with the sense of loss that I had experienced.

Leon loved watching television. In fact, left to his own devices, he would have probably watched it all day long! I have to be honest and say that I can't watch certain programmes we used to watch together. In fact, one morning – and I don't normally watch morning TV at all – I'd seen a piece of news on Twitter and I wanted to find out more, so I was looking for a news bulletin when I chanced upon an episode of *Frasier*. I had to turn if off immediately because that was one of Leon's favourite programmes, which he insisted on watching every morning. Then again, *Gogglebox* was another firm favourite!

I do still watch *Gogglebox* every week although I am not sure if I feel part of it anymore. Maybe that's not the right way of putting it. If anything, it feels as if I am visiting some old friends. I do feel as though I know these people, even though the cast have never met each other. What I feel when I watch the show now is probably the way viewers have always felt. In a way, even though I am no longer part of the show, *Gogglebox* is still a big part of me. The support I have had from Tania, Harriet, Lucy and the entire *Gogglebox* crew since Leon's passing has been remarkable. So many members of the crew have been in constant touch, even though we're not filming anymore. That to me sums up how the show really is: there's a family feeling around it. In fact, Leon and I often talked about that.

Certain members of the crew did genuinely feel like family to us but the show itself was also a programme that families watched together. That is rare in this day and age because there are so few shows where families actually gather round the television. The very idea almost seems like an antiquated concept but it's also part of the programme's continued success. In fact, that communal element is very precious, and Leon and I were extremely proud to have been part of the show's cast as a result.

On 23rd January 2018, a month after Leon's passing, *Gogglebox* won its fourth consecutive National Television Award for Best Factual Entertainment programme. The ceremony was shown on television and the actress Suranne Jones, who was presenting the award, looked skywards and said, 'God bless you, Leon', just before reading out that *Gogglebox* had won again. Leon would have loved that – he was a huge fan of Suranne Jones as he felt she was a very talented actress. Then, very kindly, sisters Ellie and Izzi Warner from Leeds, who also appear on the show, dedicated the award to Leon and me. The *Liverpool Echo* reported that the girls had said they were devastated to lose their '*Gogglebox* granddad'. It was so very kind of them. Moments like this have made me realise just how much people seem to have enjoyed what we brought to the programme.

Leon and I also worked out that the show itself represents a 16th of our life. That probably doesn't sound like that much, but if you'd been teaching in a school for five years, it would've felt like quite an achievement. Either that, or it would be time to move on! As I said at the start of this book, though, being involved in the show so late in our lives provided us with a host of unexpected pleasures.

It has also allowed me to see the good in a lot of situations, and in people in general.

Writing this book too has been an experience from which I have learnt so much. Helen and Julie both asked me how I felt about writing it and whether I felt upset, looking back at the life that Leon and I shared. I said that I didn't. Of course, it is sad that he has gone, but we had almost 58 years of married life together. If you count the five years during which we were together before that, it's over 60 years. That is quite unbelievable.

It is hard for me to remember a time when Leon wasn't in my life. I miss his generosity, his kindness, his laugher, his decisiveness, his touch and his voice – 'June!' – especially when I am out of the room. I miss him sitting in his chair with his head lost in the paper. But, most of all, I miss talking to him about all the different things we talked about. I even miss those incredibly heated discussions we used to have and which, quite often, led me to understand a different point of view ... even if Leon himself quite often refused to! It has been good to be reminded of that lifetime, full of so many adventures.

Leon once told me that when he was a child he used to dream of playing for Everton – 'I wanted to be famous and be on the back page of the *Liverpool Echo* and all of that!' He realised quite soon that he would never be a professional football player. Instead, he thought he might become a professional cricketer, that he'd play for Lancashire and be a fast left-handed bowler. The next Brian Statham, as he used to say, referring to one of his all-time cricketing heroes. When that didn't happen, he decided he would be content being married, teaching, and being a father – that was enough for him. And then, in later life and out of nowhere, *Gogglebox* came along …

Towards the end of Series Ten in late 2017, I asked Leon whether he had enjoyed the whole *Gogglebox* experience. 'I will never, ever regret having put my hand up on that Tuesday afternoon at the bridge club, June, because it has all been so much fun,' he told me.

I am not quite sure what else I can truly add to that other than to say that it really has. Our life too has been full of so many wonderful memories and so many rich experiences. Thank you, Leon. Always.

ACKNOWLEDGEMENTS

I'd like to thank Blink Publishing for giving me the opportunity to fulfil Leon's dream of writing our story. I'd also like to thank Phil Alexander, who has been on this journey with me and did so much of the research.

My gratitude to *Gogglebox* executive producer Tania Alexander and *Gogglebox* cast manager Harriet Manby, for patiently guiding me on this new venture.

I gratefully appreciate mine and Leon's wonderful friends, with whom we've shared our lives and who have given me tremendous support and care these past few months.

Last, but by no means least, my wonderful, loving, caring family, each of whom I am immensely proud of. They have brought such joy into our lives, and I cherish the time we spend together.